Praise for *I Am Not a Juvenile Delinquent*

"Sharon Charde has written a big-hearted, beautiful book, with the light touch of a poet and the deep insights of a humanist. You won't easily forget her or her girls."

—Susan Orlean, author of *The Library Book* and *The Orchid Thief*

"Charde's soulful and beautifully written book deepens our understanding of incarcerated girls and the institutions that control their lives. Woven through the narrative is Charde's own story about her difficulty managing the grief caused by the death of her son. As we read, we realize the both the author and the girls are in the midst of trauma and grieving. We understand that, at core, this is a story about despair and empowerment and, in Charde's case, a transcendent response. I recommend *I Am Not a Juvenile Delinquent* to anyone who works with girls or in detention facilities and to the much broader audience, I mean all of us, who wants to be able to turn sorrow into something meaningful."

—Mary Pipher, author of *Women Rowing North, Reviving Ophelia*, and *Writing to Change the World*

"Vulnerability. Compassion. Transparency. Inclusion, Courage. Beautiful concepts, important buzzwords, but living them is an entirely different matter. Sharon Charde has lived them. Her book, *I Am Not a Juvenile Delinquent*, is proof. In it, she maps the journey she shares with troubled girls in her writing class at a residential treatment facility. A masterful, poetic storyteller, Charde is able to break our hearts and heal them at the same time. The way she weaves the stories of her own loss and grief, with the loss and grief of the girls is stunning. What links Charde and the girls—and all of us—is the human struggle to make meaning out of trauma and spin it into the gold of transformation. Anyone who has suffered and cares about our world (that probably includes everyone) will be moved and changed by this book."

—Elizabeth Lesser, cofounder of Omega Institute and author of the New York Times bestseller *Broken Open: How Difficult Times Can Help Us Grow*, and *Marrow: Love, Loss, and What Matters Most*

"Sharon Charde, grief-stricken and adrift after the death of her son, begins leading poetry workshops at a residential treatment center for girls. Though strangers at first, the group soon forms bonds as a space for the stories of love, grief, addiction, trauma, and connection blossoms. No singular story emerges.

"Told in chronological fragments, *I Am Not a Juvenile Delinquent* is a heartfelt, emotional tribute to the transformative power of human connection. This is not an easy story. Honest, at times brutal, the stories the girls tell, and the stories Charde recounts of her relationships with the girls over a ten year period, shirk redemption. Instead, they are relentlessly raw, strong, stories that remind us both of our own powerlessness and capacity for connection. The book's power lies in that impossible, entirely true contradiction. I loved it."

—Tessa Fontaine, author of *The Electric Woman: A Memoir in Death-Defying Acts*

"This stunning memoir, written with the eye, ear and imagery of a poet, takes the reader through a grieving mother's journey toward healing—as she reaches out to others who, like her, have been shattered by unspeakable grief. Charde encourages young incarcerated women to find their voices and to write and share their haunting life stories, as she shares hers with them. A testament to the healing power of writing, *I Am Not a Juvenile Delinquent* shows us that

lead can be alchemized into gold when we trust enough to share our
deepest secrets on the page."

—Carol Henderson, author of *Losing Malcolm: A Mother's Journey
Through Grief* and *Farther Along: The Writing Journey of Thirteen
Bereaved Mothers*

"Poet and memoirist Sharon Charde, having grieved for eight years
the mysterious death of her young son, goes into a residence for
girls paroled for drug addiction, to write with them. Writing together
in order to heal the troubled young women, Charde finds healing
happening within herself: '...these girls showed me the stranger
of myself, the locked up one who'd longed to spring free...these
delinquent girls called bad by the world...would soon become the
definition of real to me.' She takes us close inside the girl's lives. To
read *I Am Not a Juvenile Delinquent* is to find oneself one of 'the girls,'
and then to realize their journey is also the reader's own. Go there
with her; you, too, will be changed."

—Pat Schneider, author of *Writing Alone and with Others* and *How the
Light Gets In: Writing as a Spiritual Practice* and founder of Amherst
Writers & Artists

"Sharon Charde has written an eye-opener of a book about listening
to the youthful missteps that shape our lives while reflecting on how
they shape our futures. She gives the reader an unflinching look at
her subjects—her Touchstone Girls—that shows her love, respect, and
deep frustration in an unjust world as she reflects her optimism and
fears for them in an open-hearted yet realistic way.

"Workshopping with her over an intense decade, her poetry students
guide her to the dark side of the world of drugs, rape, incest, and
poverty...forcing the author to come to grips with every parent's
worst nightmare—the loss of a child due to addiction, violence, and
in her own agonizing case, the unsolved cause of death of her newly

adult son. Written with sparkling retrospection and a plain-spoken honesty, *I Am Not a Juvenile Delinquent* is a book to be trusted, valued, and shared."

—Glen Finland, author of *Next Stop: A Memoir of Family*

"Sharon Charde's writing about trauma grabs us and forces us to feel what we most want to avoid feeling. She brings us back to feeling and thereby back to a fuller life."

—Jessica Stern, bestselling author of *My War Criminal, Denial, Terror in the Face of God,* and *ISIS*

"Sharon Charde explores how grief gives way to insight even when healing cannot happen and voids cannot be filled. Her crystalline writing offers glimpses of hope in unlikely places. She paints a vivid picture of how connecting with others, however different they may be, can be a step toward making a whole life. It is a worthy portrait of her own."

—Mary E. Hunt, Co-Director, Women's Alliance for Theology, Ethics, and Ritual (WATER)

"Sharon Charde's delicate strength, her affection for her students (and theirs for her), her passion for the power and influence of poetry, will enrich any reader's life, as it has the lives of the young women she inspired. Her new book should be required reading for everyone. It is marvelous."

—Abigail Thomas, author of *Safekeeping, A Three Dog Life, What Comes Next and How to Like It*

I Am Not a
Juvenile
Delinquent

I Am Not a
Juvenile
Delinquent

How Poetry Changed a Group of
At-Risk Young Women

SHARON CHARDE

CORAL GABLES

...for every one of my girls, always.

For permission requests, please contact the publisher at:
Mango Publishing Group
2850 S Douglas Road, 2nd Floor
Coral Gables, FL 33134 USA
info@mango.bz

For special orders, quantity sales, course adoptions and corporate sales, please email the publisher at sales@mango.bz. For trade and wholesale sales, please contact Ingram Publisher Services at customer.service@ingramcontent.com or +1.800.509.4887.

I Am Not a Juvenile Delinquent: How Poetry Changed a Group of At-Risk Young Women

LCCN: 2020933918

BISAC: SOC032000—SOCIAL SCIENCE / Gender Studies

Printed in the United States of America

Each day, we're given many opportunities to open up or shut down. The most precious opportunity presents itself when we come to the place where we think we can't handle whatever is happening. It's too much. It's gone too far... There's no way we can manipulate the situation to make ourselves come out looking good... Basically, life has just nailed us.

It's as if you just looked at yourself in a mirror and saw a gorilla. The mirror's there; it's showing you, and what you see looks bad. You try to angle the mirror so you will look a little better, but no matter what you do, you still look like a gorilla. That's being nailed by life, the place where you have no choice but to embrace what's happening or push it away.

—Pema Chodron, *When Things Fall Apart*

It's not like I'm some whole person trying to help the broken people I see along the road. I think I am broken by the injustice I see.

—Bryan Stevenson

Table of Contents

Part I

Initiate

Part II

My Girls

Part 3

Turning Point

Cast of Characters

PROGRAM DIRECTORS

Lori
Michelle
Beka

TOUCHSTONE STAFF

Lesley
Hiram
Angel
Briana
Donna
Kaneisha
Jess
Lindsay
Carol
Vernell
Denise

GIRLS IN EARLY GROUPS

Kaylee
Mayra
Alondra
Brisa
Ana
Nia
La Toya
Tiffany
Nadia

Isabella
Melanie
Ellie
Rontae (later, in
the documentary)

FEATURED GIRLS

Tarray
Chimere
Jeni
Miranda
Molly

HOTCHKISS STUDENTS

Lacey
Carla
Becca
Brady
Caroline
Lois

TOUCHSTONE GIRLS IN HOTCHKISS GROUP

Kimani
Molly
Miranda

Ja'Keria
Dominique
Marissa

HOTCHKISS TEACHERS

Nancy
Athena

BOSTON TRIP GIRLS

Molly
Miranda
Ja'Keria
Artrese
Dominique

OTHERS

Sister Benedicta (my mentor as a young woman)
Cecile (Tarray's grandmother)
Suzanne (Danbury High teacher)
Stewart Wilson (Artwell director)
Brian Judd (TV interviewer)
Dennis Watlington (one of first African American students at the
Hotchkiss school)
Pam (Hartford Academy liason)
Denise (Tarray's mentor for the Sunken Garden performance)
Jon Baskin (documentary filmmaker)
Matthew (my son)
John (my husband)

Foreword

What pulls any of us to do this kind of work? It can be hard to trace the source of such a fierce call, although Sharon—in the aftermath of her son's death and the closing of her family therapy practice—clearly sought new direction and meaning for her life. And despite the roadblocks, second guessing, and myriad other challenges along the way, it is undeniably true that writing with women who have been caught in "the system" as a result of all kinds of abuse and addiction can be both humbling and healing. In the right hands, layers of need and fulfillment manifest in process, product, and belonging. As Sharon wrote, "things don't go away; they become you."

And so the world of young women she worked with at Touchstone became Sharon's. Like anyone entering the uniquely chaotic world of justice-involved institutions, she quickly acclimated to the physical restraints of locked doors; the constant chatter among those charged with keeping order; the unpredictability of schedules, staff, and group members; the challenging borders between plan and execution. And beneath it all, she gently midwifed the deep expressiveness that the girls soon enough learned to share in a safe and confidential space set apart in the otherwise regimented and restricted environment. She learned the rules and how to bend them to support each young woman's emerging voice. She put herself in front of them week after week, for two hours, at her own volition and out of her own love for writing which soon enough morphed into love for these struggling young women.

One of the more humbling experiences of holding writing space in such a setting—once you have "proven" yourself by showing up again and again, regardless of whether any group members do; by acting consistently, showing mutual respect; and treating each story/voice as worthy of engaged listening—is the mutual enrichment of shared stories from such different worlds. Sharon was wise to keep putting "her" girls' stories before wider outside audiences. I know from our Vermont readings, audiences were consistently awed by the power of these women's voices, their courage, their determination to grow and change. As Sharon wrote elsewhere, "I pull words from a deeper place, feelings from behind doors I didn't know were closed. I face fears and change, look into mirrors side by side with the girls in my writing group." It is impossible to do this work with authenticity and not be deeply affected by it. And slowly, in the unlikeliest of places, mutual healing begins.

Perhaps the most difficult part of these intense sessions is how attached the facilitator becomes to the group members. Beyond the logistical concerns and manipulations to make the program work—and they are considerable, involving a seemingly endless learning curve filled with sharp turns and reversals—this deeper connection is what can keep us going for ten years, week after week after week. You identify with those "empty spaces that yearn for fullness" and learn from "the certainty of impermanence, the folly of desiring things to be other than how they are." You struggle to hold firm the boundaries between them and all the former versions of yourself that keep popping up in their/your writing. You, as Sharon says, "want to spring us all out of prison and into freedom with the magic of writing... to change the world, their worlds, my world, the world of our bigger communities, with our loud, wild voices."

But there *are* boundaries, bigger and more forbidding than the barbed wire of a physical prison or the locked doors of the heart, or the reach of one woman's passionate vision. While inside, the young women have enough structure to get them to classes, assigned jobs, therapy, even writing group. Once outside, you can only provide so much incentive, facilitation, cheerleading, and other personal resources. At some point you, too, need to learn to let go. You can't, as Sharon says, "keep wanting for them if they didn't want for themselves." And so, after ten brave and incredibly rich years, she was able to step back and evaluate the balance between what she could offer and what she needed, knowing she had gained what she came for through all she had given of herself, her time, her talents. There can be no greater gift to her struggling writers; no firmer path to their mutual growth. At some point, each of us must move onward—even with the occasional backward step. And as both Sharon and I can tell you, a wealth of these girls-become-women will remain active in our hearts and our lives well into the future.

Sarah Bartlett
Westport, MA

● ● ●

In 2010, Sarah W. Bartlett created *writinginsideVT* for Vermont's incarcerated women to write for personal and social change within a supportive community. She co-edited two collections of their writings. *Hear Me, See Me: Incarcerated Women Write* (Orbis Books, 2013) and *LifeLines: Re-Writing Lives from Inside Out* (Green Writers Press, 2019). Learn more at: https://writinginsidevt.com/.

Introduction

It wasn't very long after I began volunteering at Touchstone that I began taking notes on our sessions, forcing myself to record everything that had happened each day as soon as I got home. Meeting with the girls (as I affectionately call them), dealing with the staff and administration, finding pertinent prompts and material, all held so much emotion, power, and drama that I must have somehow known there was a bigger story there, even though that idea was certainly not at the forefront of my mind at the time. I just knew I had to get the details, the dialogue, the anecdotes—all of it—scribbled into my red notebook, or typed hurriedly on my computer, exhausted or not.

With no paradigm to follow, I had to make one up. And revise what I'd planned more often than not, as the girls challenged my every strategy. After many sessions, I realized I had to start typing up their work so they could see what amazing poets they truly were. I brought in plastic folders so they could gather their poems into a collection, and this delighted them. Fortunately, I had the presence of mind to eventually get them to sign publication releases, imagining the creation of an anthology of their work one day, which I did publish in 2005.

So all the details in *I Am Not A Juvenile Delinquent* are as close as possible to what actually happened in our sessions, public readings, and other time together. The young women, Touchstone staff members, Hotchkiss teachers, students, and others you will read about are real, and most have given consent to use their actual names, though a few have been changed for various reasons.

But there is much not told, many young women not written about, many poems still in files in cabinets and my computer, as ten years is a long time. I wish you could know them all, these splendid, courageous, profound human beings. I wish you could know more of what they've endured as girls in "the system," in their homes, classrooms, and neighborhoods. I wish you could know them now, women in their twenties and thirties, raising children, trying to make it in this troubled world, determined to give those children the best of themselves, struggling to make it with their partners.

I want you to know their humanity, their beauty, their gifts, without the cruel labels assigned to them by society. I want you to know how unsurprising it is that they've been incarcerated for doing what they did—selling and using drugs, truancy, assault, prostitution, running away—in most cases, to survive impossible situations. I want you to know how much they have to offer the world.

Perhaps this book can elucidate some of those things; I hope so.

But what I can tell you is this: those young women saved me. And my gratitude for them, each and every one, is immeasurable. This book is a small expression of that gratitude. Thank you, my dearest, dearest girls.

Sharon Charde
Lakeville, CT
January 28, 2020

Part I

Initiate

"I am always doing things I can't do.
That's how I get to do them."
—Pablo Picasso

Fish Tank

I was wild, raw, still crazed with grief twelve years after my son had fallen from a wall in Rome and died alone in the night. Despite the details gleaned from the embassy and investigation, the autopsy, his teachers in the junior year abroad program, and the friend who was with him that night, his death continued to be an unsolved mystery in my mind. I thought I'd tried everything possible to heal myself—becoming a shaman, falling in love with a woman, writing poetry, traveling the world, going to therapy, living alone on an island for nine months, meditating long hours on Buddhist retreats. But my world continued crumbled and unredeemed. My husband and I grieved differently, so often found it difficult to offer the comfort we so badly needed to each other.

I was stuck in a black hole, blind and dumb, staring at what Pema Chodron, esteemed Buddhist scholar and teacher, called "the gorilla in the mirror."

Me.

I couldn't bear what I saw.

Someone, maybe one of my therapy clients, gave me a book, *Ophelia Speaks*, a collection of first-person pieces written by teen girls. I ripped through it, remembering the inner-city girls I'd taught so long ago, my adolescent clients, and how I'd loved them. The girls in the book— their pain felt like my pain, somehow. And they were writing about it, pouring out their stories as I'd been prompting the women in my writing workshops to do.

Around the same time I heard about Touchstone, a residential treatment center for young women that had opened up in a town not too far from mine. I thought, *Maybe I could go there, volunteer myself, start a group, get the girls to write about their lives ?* I called the place and talked with the director about my idea. We agreed to meet the following week.

• • •

I pulled into a small parking lot across from an impressive stone mansion. *This must be Touchstone*, I thought, startled to see such a non-institutional-looking building. Suddenly chilly in the Indian summer heat, I pushed the buzzer at the locked front door several times before someone came. A strikingly pretty and very young woman opened it, a little out of breath.

"Hi, I'm Lori," she said, looking at me questioningly. It was almost fifteen minutes past the time I'd promised to arrive on this mid-September day in 1999.

"I got a bit lost," I said. "So sorry to be late."

"No problem," she said, "Come on in, I've got to make lunch for the kids. We can talk while I cook."

Lori led me past the stairs she'd just run down, through a dismal room housing a bunch of brown wooden tables and chairs—a dining room, maybe—to a big business-like kitchen full of stainless steel. She opened the oven of the enormous commercial stove to slide in several baking sheets full of frozen tater tots. Corn was heating up on the gas burner in a big pot. There was no one else in sight.

"They're at school," she said, hearing the question in my mind. "They'll come up for lunch around 12:30. So we can talk until then."

I was confused. Why was the director making lunch? Why was she so impossibly young? I didn't know then how great the director turnover would be at Touchstone. The facility had just opened a few years ago, and was a fledgling attempt at the first all-female residential treatment center in Connecticut. Gayle Brooks, a long-time Department of Children and Families senior staff member, who'd believed in gender-sensitive treatment rather than punitive incarceration for young women in trouble with the law, had looked for a piece of Connecticut real estate that might be appropriate for a small pilot program for these girls. The North American Family Institute had purchased this fifty-seven-acre property, a former psychiatric institution for the wealthy, in the prosperous country town of Litchfield.

Lori had begun working here as a staff member right after college. She later told me three residents had locked her in a closet the first year, that no one had really known quite what they were doing, and that it had been the daily crises that had educated the young staff on how to figure out a program and structure that could contain the obstreperous girls. She'd been made director just recently, at twenty-six.

Lori and I sat at one of the wooden dining tables inset with blue Formica. The day was hot and there was no air-conditioning. I was surprised at her outfit, a light tank top and capris, having imagined a director who wore a suit or dress.

"Gee, you're looking nice and cool in this heat," I said.

"Oh, we're pretty casual around here," she said, pulling off a scrunchie and remaking her blonde ponytail.

I put out my CV and some writing retreat brochures on the table, feeling I needed to authenticate myself. She didn't look down.

"I've been doing writing workshops with women for years," I said, a little fast. "I'd really like to try working with teen girls, and I've always wanted to work with the incarcerated. Um, I'd volunteer, of course," I added hastily.

"Well, what exactly do you want to do?" she asked. *Here it comes,* I thought. *She won't like the idea, or will say it couldn't work here.* I sat up straighter, trying to look more serious.

"Well, um, I thought I would meet with all the girls, do a sample presentation of what I'd like to do each week with them, you know, get them to write, and then see who wants to be part of a weekly writing group."

"That sounds fine. Why don't you come next Monday after school, around 3:00? How long do you think it will take to do one group?"

"Well, I'm not sure. Maybe an hour, hour and a half?"

"Okay, we'll do it all in a day, then. We'll try two groups of ten girls each. All right? I've got to get those tater tots out before they burn."

"Sure, okay, fine, Lori. So I'll come here at 3:00, then, on Monday?"

Somehow I had thought we'd talk longer, that she would have wanted to know more about exactly what I would do, about me, question me further. That our meeting would have been more, well, official.

"Yes, we'll meet in the living room, right across the way. See you then."

"Do you think I could look at the room before I leave?" I could feel her desire to move on to the next task, but I was compelled to stay longer, to get more of a sense of the place, prepare myself for the meeting with the young women I hadn't really been sure she'd agree to. Suddenly, it seemed what I'd hoped for so impulsively was going to actually happen.

"Sure," she said, "It's right across the hall." She pulled open a heavy metal door and gestured towards the large dark room. A gurgling fish tank sat in a corner, and a bunch of scruffy chairs were scattered about on the rugless floor. A massive fireplace, remnant of a time when this had been someone's home, dominated the shadowy space. It seemed as oddly out of place as I was.

"Take a look; I've got to go, the girls will be coming up soon." Lori smiled and shook my damp hand, turned and went back to the kitchen.

I stood in there staring at the fish tank. It contained a large, solitary orange fish that swam in slow, rhythmic circles.

It had seemed too easy, getting Lori to say yes to my idea. I hadn't had to offer any credentials, tell her I'd worked as a therapist for twenty years, was a published poet.

As I stood there staring at the fish, working with this group of girls began to seem like an unthinkable task. Suddenly I wasn't at all sure I wanted to do this new thing that might actually shift the focus of my life out from under its leaden coat of mourning. After all, nothing else had worked. "Mother of a dead son" had become my definition, the pain that weighted my days a connection to my son I was unwilling to surrender.

I remembered Buddhist teacher Pema Chodron's gorilla in the mirror. It was hard to look at mine. How could I face a whole roomful of tough, suspicious girls and keep myself together? They would probably see right through me, a gray-haired white woman so much older than they were, trying to get some distraction from her own pain. Maybe there was no way I was ready to do this.

I walked back to my car, stomach caved in on itself, head clanging. When I opened the door, I dropped my bag, everything spilling out onto the cracked and heaving pavement of the parking lot.

First Meeting

It was another really hot afternoon, that first meeting day. But the big room was surprisingly cool, with its non-matching shabby chairs and couches, a dark rug now on the floor. The fish tank still gurgled. The room was dim, almost murky. There were only two floor lamps to light the large space.

I waited alone, shivering a bit in my standard summer and fall "uniform" of that era: a white t-shirt, black capris, and black slides.

A queue of girls, accompanied by several staff, marched in and sat down on chairs lined up against the wall. Their skin was of various shades of white, black, and tan. Mostly they were dressed in very tight jeans, tank tops, and t-shirts. They looked like regular teenagers. They all had fascinating hairdos—spiked or dyed red, braided into cornrows or gelled into long corkscrew curls. Most of them wore sneakers or flip-flops, and large gold hoop earrings.

They were, to a one, beautiful.

"Hi girls, I'm Sharon Charde," I blurted out, my voice probably too loud. "It's really exciting to be meeting with you. I read this great book, *Ophelia Speaks*, full of stories about different lives written by girls like you, and thought maybe I'd come and see if some of you might want to be part of a group that could do that too."

They were silent, blankly staring straight ahead, bored-looking. Sure that this crazy idea of mine would never work, I kept talking—what I always did when I was anxious— trying to pull their interest from its locked-up place.

"The world needs to hear your important stories. I want to try to help you tell them. What we do won't be 'school writing', but writing from the heart, what is true and real in your lives, what you're thinking, feeling, and struggling with."

"Miss," one of them called out, "I can't write."

"What?" I said. "Everyone can write, it's okay," thinking she'd meant she couldn't write well.

One of the staff spoke up and said her words were true, that she was disabled and really couldn't write.

"Support!" the girls chorused. I later found out this was a kind of all-purpose word used frequently for all sorts of reasons, but actually did feel very supportive.

"Okay. That's okay. You can listen." I turned to the girl who said she was unable to write and smiled. She gazed into the space just beyond me. I smiled harder, trying to meet her eyes. She didn't look any different from the other girls. Finally, she gave me a wan grin. The small triumph made me feel a little braver.

"So let's try to write today in the same way we'll write in the group. So you can see if you'd be interested. There will be some rules," I said. "Important rules."

A staff member interrupted me to tell me they had no "rules" at Touchstone, but "expectations."

"Okay." I corrected myself. "Expectations."

"Here's the first one—you can't write freely unless you feel safe. In order to make sure we are all safe, everyone needs to make some commitments—to confidentiality, number one. No talking about anyone else's writing here or outside the group. Second, silence when someone is reading what she's written. Next, no comments afterwards, no questions. No writing about anyone else in the group. If it's too hard to read, ask someone else to read it for you, or I will. And finally, everyone needs to write, even staff members and definitely me."

The staff members demurred on this last one. I let it go. The group hadn't officially formed and I wanted to make my idea a reality too badly to derail the conversation. I didn't yet know how thick the lines were supposed to be between the young women and staff.

"If you don't like what I suggest, you can always write about something else. So let's start."

I knew I had to go for broke this first time. So I read a piece from *Voices From The Hood*, a booklet put out by a Chicopee, Massachusetts, teen writing group from "the projects" that had been started by an organization called Amherst Writers and Artists.

The story was about a girl whose drug-addicted mother killed her dog Pal because the girl hadn't done what her mother wanted fast enough. It was a horribly painful account of violence and profound betrayal.

Staff members handed out paper and pens.

I asked the girls to relate a similar painful experience in their lives. To my surprise, most of them immediately focused on the writing. Heads down, pens working the paper, they wrote with absorption. Many volunteered to read, sharing stories just as horrible or worse.

"I would come home from school looking for my mom and find her in the garage lighting up a crack pipe," one girl wrote.

"My mother wouldn't believe me when I told her I'd been raped for seven years," another read.

Still another told us, "I remember having my baby, how much it hurt."

"Support!" the girls called out to each reader.

Another girl, Kaylee, had written that her mother was just like the one in the story I'd read. "I wish she'd never lay down with my father," she read from a notebook. "I hate her."

Afterwards she told me how good it had felt to have written and read the piece, but that a lot of emotion had been stirred up in her. I worried that she'd have no place to go with it, but then remembered Lori had told me in a follow-up call that these girls had weekly clinical groups and "advocates" on the staff with whom they could talk.

"Thank you for coming, miss. I want to join your group," Kaylee asserted. "It will be good for me." Her eyes met mine in total openness. "I cut off my bracelets, that's how I got here."

"Bracelets?" I was puzzled.

"You know, when you're in jail at home you have to wear them."

No, I didn't know, but found out later from Lori that they were ankle cuffs that monitored the girls in home jail and beeped loudly when they left the prescribed space. Kaylee had worn them because she had broken her curfew too many times.

The dark room felt alive now, coursing with words and feelings and hands waving for recognition. I was reminded of my first teaching job, of the ineptness I'd felt in the unfamiliar land of a cavernous inner-city school. But I also remembered the surges of delight and connection I'd experienced in those classrooms stuffed full of restless adolescents in blue jumpers and white blouses.

Now, everything in me yearned to stay with these hurting, tough girls— to give them whatever I could. I hoped the staff and director would want me to come back. I hoped some more girls would want to join the group.

I'd been there almost three hours. It was 5:45 when I left, and all the way home I felt filled to my edges with a warmth and recognition in a way I hadn't in so very long.

And it wasn't only my experiences with my previous students that the young women at Touchstone called forth. It was my adolescent self, though that would take a long time to grasp. I'd always been a disciplined person; I'd spent my adolescence in what had felt like a kind of jail, a convent school in West Hartford, Connecticut. The strict limits of my Catholic life had been so confining that outside exploration had seemed impossible. Clothed and shod each day in a baggy navy dress and blue-and-white saddle shoes, I'd studied religion and French, English and Latin, getting top grades. I'd been editor of the school paper, had had a leading role in the senior play, sung in the glee club, been a Foreign Policy representative and debate club president, written essays that won Scholastic writing awards. I'd gone to a Catholic girls' camp every summer where I'd been captain of my team, received awards for leadership, camp spirit, and mountaineering.

That's who I thought I was.

But these girls showed me the stranger within me, the locked-up one who'd longed to spring free of the confines and limitations of my upbringing. I'd never done anything more forbidden than smoking in the woods behind my cabin at camp or wearing lipstick before I was sixteen. I'd wanted to, but had been too afraid of sin and punishment, the disapproval of my parents and teachers, of what breaking out would mean to my regimented life. So they were a fascination, "the other," these at-risk girls labeled "bad" by the world, who would soon become the definition of *real* to me.

If I Could, I Would

"Miss, you dress in style for an old lady," said Kaylee when we gathered for our first meeting a week later. "Look at those shoes!"

"You're going to read us a story today, aren't you?" she said with eager excitement. "I really liked that story you read us about Pal. I couldn't stop thinking about it."

"Yes, I'm going to read you a story each time we meet," I said. I'd gone through my books at home searching for stories these girls might connect with, and could see I'd have a large task ahead of me—to find books and poetry relevant to their lives instead of the lives of the middle-class white women I'd been teaching— instead of my own.

Six of them decided they wanted to be in my first group. Lori called to tell me, and set a regular time for me to come in, Mondays at 3:15. She came down to the dorm basement with them that first day, giving each girl a notebook. Nia, stunning and beautifully dressed, with an hourglass figure; Mayra, who would write almost every week about her mother, in an agony of desire to be seen by a woman who had never been there for her; Brisa, who would write little and talk less; and Ana, who would sleep through most of our sessions, were seated along with mature-looking, sensual La Toya, and Kaylee, the girl who cut her bracelets and the only Caucasian.

I had a piece today from *Ophelia Speaks*, about a girl's fantasy of love—her boyfriend had died from shooting up drugs. I'd hoped it would resonate, and asked them to write a girl-boy story. Mayra looked around the room before she read her piece—"This is confidential, right?" I assured her it was, and reminded the group of the importance of keeping what was said in the room stays in the room.

Shit Is Happening

weed was my girl
Mary Jane was my girl
if I had a problem
I couldn't understand
we all need Mary to lean on
she was my main thang
she made my heart sing

that's what I thought about the ganja
used to wake up smoking
go to bed smoking
five blunts to the head

to go to a party
before I left
had to smoke
when I got there
I had to smoke

couldn't even sell weed
'cause I would smoke it all
so I sold crack
go to NY with my boy
get some kilos
smoking by myself
taking a shit smoking
smoking with my man
turning into a monster

if you didn't have my money
you was getting hurt
always remember my mom saying
where you getting all that money?
my brothers, my man
didn't know I was selling crack

they always asking
where you getting all that money?
how you getting all

that money?
me leaving my house
didn't come back four or five days
then at 5:00 in the morning
Ma stressed out, worried
police chasing me
my boyz called me fugitive
got into a fight every time

I smoked weed
used to drive my boyz
when they was drunk
used to go to a motel
my girl and me always
at the club

my girl got raped
we slashed that nigga's tires
messed up his car
he couldn't go nowhere
me and my boy chilled with blunts
like they was cigarettes

we watch *Flubber*
was rolling off that movie
day later they raided my boyz
my man TJ
all went to jail
same day my boy scared
shot this dude because
he gave him five dollars instead of twenty

I was out
my girls went to her crib
ten minutes later somebody do a drive-by
we was all on the floor
shit just happenin' tonight

In jeans and the usual tight tank top, she looked at all of us with satisfaction. "He tried to break my neck, but I still love him" Mayra said. "It's so special how he runs his fingers through my hair. Like this," she

I Am Not a Juvenile Delinquent

reached up to slither her hand through her gelled black locks. "I miss my Mary Jane," she sighed. "It felt good to write about her. Those were some crazy times."

* * *

We did three prompts that afternoon. For the next one, I'd brought in a bag of objects: an onion, a pink razor with a flower motif, a child's toy school bus, a jar of cinnamon, a lipstick. The woman staff member on duty with us that day wrote a moving piece about the razor—the flowers and the blade, the two ways you could go in life, the loss of innocence that came with shaving your legs for the first time. The girls were fascinated, especially because staff members were not supposed to reveal personal information to the girls, that heavy black line. I knew it was a good rule, but one that needed to be broken at least partially in our group if we were all to write with honesty.

"If I Could, I Would," was the final prompt suggestion, and they just took off. Mayra wanted to be the ocean, Ana, a bird that flew away and a Bengal tiger.

"Do you know what *that* is?" she asks, looking hard at me.

"Yes, I do, Ana," I said, meeting her gaze firmly.

Brisa wrote of wanting her dead brother back and Kaylee of wanting to be with her mother, taking away the meanness in her. Kaylee seemed so young, so innocent, so adorable, that it was hard to get myself to believe she'd done anything lawless.

They all wrote of giving the homeless homes, the poor money, of wanting out of the projects. The room coursed with energy. I was elated. When I got home that night I couldn't stop talking, telling my husband John every detail of the afternoon's meeting.

Smiling, he wrapped his arms around me. "Those girls are lucky to have you," he said.

But I already knew I was the lucky one.

Facials, Confrontations, Advocates

The guiding principle for daily life at Touchstone was called "the normative model." It was a behavioral conditioning template that employed a mission statement, specific language for various misbehaviors, expectations, and penalties for "going off mission."

The model was predicated on a level system. When the girls were admitted they were on level one, not allowed to leave the facility and with very few privileges. Level five was the top, achieved by very few; those who made it were allowed the freedom to walk around the campus with their own walkie-talkies—like the ones carried by all staff. Most of the girls see-sawed between levels two and three—three, allowed off-grounds access, two was still restricted. At weekly community meetings, staff members and the whole group of young women would vote on whether or not the person who was "going for her level" should be given the privilege she sought.

• • •

"Yo, I'm confronting you, you did a boundary violation, I saw you kissin' her in the house bathroom last night."

"That's a facial, girl, no way you gettin' away with that."

It was humorous to hear these young women tossing the Touchstone lingo into their ordinary conversations. A boundary violation meant any physical touch. The "facial" was not a beauty treatment but a grimace, a roll of the eyes, or some look that could be understood as a challenge to fight, an insult, or some other troublesome communication. Many of the girls were so volatile and had so little impulse control that a "facial" could start a major assault.

"You off mission, girl. Get you feet off the couch. You s'posed to be in group now, get goin'."

A "confrontation" could be made by holding up a hand in the shape of the letter "C." A staff member would then call on the girl to make her confrontation. Everyone in the area would then singsong "the mission," which was "making responsible choices within our community."

To me, the behavioral model's rote jargon made them sound like absurd parrots. I questioned whether this stilted and inauthentic language was going to be helpful to them when they reentered the outside world.

Over the next weeks, I began to realize how new the residential facility and its concept was, but wasn't sure what to expect from staff members. I discovered all did not have college degrees and counseling experience or at least courses; I'd presumed they did. I'd assumed that their mission in life would be to care for these wounded girls with compassion and concern, and that they would all be female.

Oh, was I wrong.

There were at least as many males as females on staff, if not more, and though it seemed strange to me that men would be involved with young women in such an intimate way— for example, standing outside bathroom doors while they showered— I slowly understood that there could never be enough women to fill the required positions. I also came to know that many of the girls did not trust women, and related much better to males, which surprised me, given the destruction I learned anew every week that had been done to them by the men in their lives.

The pay was lamentable for the hard work and long hours required (maybe twelve dollars an hour at that time), the geographical location was far from cities that would have a larger pool of available hires, and there were just not a lot of people who wanted a job like this.

And these deeply scarred girls were difficult if not impossible much of the time, sometimes even physically abusive, both to each other and to staff. And I would later see that staff turnover was continual, which seemed destabilizing to me.

The staff members were called advocates and were assigned a number of girls who were called their "advocatees." The advocates were supposed to be available as needed for frequent talks and support, but the reality was that they were usually too busy putting out the constant fires that burned high and hot in a facility like this.

Facials, Confrontations, Advocates

And they cut me no slack, this new intruder into their formulaic days. One staff member's eyes would blaze at me when I saw her in the hall. She would move protectively towards the girls she was herding to their next activity, and shout angrily for silence or make a confrontation if one called out, "Hi, Miss Sharon!" or "How you doin', miss?" pushing them past me. Another named Hiram turned the other way when he saw me coming, and still another one would refuse to answer my questions if he was assigned to the group.

I didn't yet understand why I was meeting such opposition.

I was required to have a staff person with me at all times when I was with the girls, and I prayed I would have none of the ones that seemed so opposed to me. Since the person would vary each week depending on who was working that day, I never knew whom I would get. I felt we really needed a female to preserve the group's intimacy. Lori agreed, but the difficulties of who was available when, who'd called in sick, whether or not there was a crisis on the floor, made scheduling a particular person seemingly impossible.

The girls were not allowed to swear or use street slang in the program, but I had insisted to Lori that when they wrote with me they needed that freedom so that their poems and stories would be free from self-censorship and could flow freely. She agreed, but many of the staff frowned upon this, and actually a few of the girls would find it difficult as well.

I was pushing liberation in a place that held its inhabitants captive.

Sun Porch

I thought about the girls all the time: in the car, in the shower, walking in the woods. I talked to my husband about them incessantly. He listened patiently, understanding how important this new work was becoming to me, though with some concern about how wholly I'd given myself to it.

I had been accustomed to my therapy clients' painful histories, but what these girls had put forth in a few weeks trumped those stories with their raw truths.

I was falling into their lives.

The sheer amount of what these girls had suffered was eclipsing my own anguish. Our meetings were the heart of my week. Their poems spoke of such brokenness and abuse by those who were supposed to care for them, teachers, parents, relatives, and boyfriends, stories that stunned me and often brought me to tears. But because the whole project was a work in progress, I had not yet begun the practice of typing up their pieces every week and saving them on my computer, so I do not have many from this time.

* * *

"La Toya, your hair looks so great today!"

"Sharon, I'm Nia, not La Toya! Can't you remember our names right?"

"Oh God, I'm so sorry, Nia and La Toya. Can you forgive me?"

"Of course," Nia laughed and hugged me.

Only five of the group had shown up. One was on a medical pass and another was on the run. She'd gone AWOL and they hadn't been able to find her. I'd chosen a prompt about mothers for today with both of them in mind. *Oh well*, I thought, *that prompt will work for anyone.*

We gathered wherever the staff found room for us, and the sun porch was the only place available for our meeting today. I was seeing that trying to plan anything—a meeting place, the amount of time we could spend, what girls would be available to come, even the prompts themselves—was impossible. I protested to our assigned staff, but as I would eventually learn, I just had to make do with whatever room was unengaged that day.

The sun porch was an open space off the dining room with a big table in the middle for overflow. It was also a storage space for random stuff packed in plastic tubs and a passageway to the outside, so people walked in and out all the time. It lacked privacy and it was quite cool in seasons other than summer, when the glass windows made it extremely hot. It could hardly have been less appropriate as a gathering place for our new group and the safe space I'd promised them.

"I'm so sorry, girls. We have to get a better place to meet. I'll talk to Lori. Who wants to read first?"

"I'm not going to read, Nia is not showing respect," Mayra said sullenly, throwing her a facial.

Nia had begun talking with Ana, the girl who'd wanted to be a Bengal tiger, about something that had happened last night. I agreed that she was not following our group expectations and reminded her of that.

"Okay, okay, calm down, miss," she said. Nia always had something to say. She pushed even farther the wide boundaries I set in our group, clearly a young woman used to getting her own way and often erupting when she didn't. I thought she liked our meetings, but she was often sullen and exasperating.

Mayra's piece was a passionate imploration to her mother to love her, notice her. She was so sensitive, so smart, so perceptive. I wondered how she could ever overcome all the trauma she'd experienced.

Dear Ma,

I just want you to know I love you. You say you love me, but do you really? I feel like I'm standing alone in the darkness. I really wish that I could trust you and have that bond with you, like the way you felt when I was born.

I feel pain in my heart. I feel abandoned. I know that's a big word, but if you were here and were proud of your baby girl, then I wouldn't cry all night and call myself a stupid bitch for

I Am Not a Juvenile Delinquent

messing up. Picture how you would feel if I died. Would you cry, or would you wipe the dust off your shoulders and keep walking?

I love you so much, I love you more than myself. But you don't understand that I'm trying to do the right things. I've changed, and I want you to know I'm sorry for what I did wrong, but stop blaming me and my brothers for your husband's death. We didn't kill him. He killed himself. Why did you let him beat on you or beat on us, why did you tell him you loved him, why did you pick him over us, why did you believe that he loved you?

Ma, there are so many things I want to tell you but I can't, because the family will fall apart. I mean, when Jenito touched me, nobody believed me but you, but do you believe that I love you, do you know who I am, what my favorite food is? Why does my father not love me? How come he can't spell my name right? How come you told the policeman to take me, said that they could have me, is that when you stopped loving me?

So think, if you was me and I was you how would you feel, how would it be? Can we have a bond, or are we going to fall apart?

Kaylee wrote eloquently of her hatred for her mother, but quickly moved on to her boyfriend.

"He wants me to go naked, free. I'm not ready to give him the best thing I have, but I cried when I told him no."

Kaylee was just fourteen. A petite Caucasian, the only one in the group, she was such a pretty girl, slim and agile, with a clean, clear, expressive face, her blonde hair pulled back tightly in a scrunchie.

"Can we talk about virginity, Sharon?" she wanted to know.

"Kaylee, that is an important subject, a really big one, but we just don't have time today. Maybe next week I'll give a prompt and we can write about it."

Based on what they'd shared to date, I didn't think any of the other girls were virgins, and was wary about such a conversation and how they would react.

"Girls, I thought our next piece could be a letter to yourself as a little girl. Tell her who you are now and how she helped you to get where you are—or anything else you want to say to her. Let's try it, okay?"

"No, no, Sharon, we don't like that, we don't want to go there," Nia and Mayra said together. This was another surprise to me. It took time to understand how threatening it could be for some of them, most of them, to dip into the past. Recalling the traumas of their younger years was often unbalancing and frightening, though the girls that stayed in the group for a sustained period of time got much braver with looking back, even eager to do so. I would encourage them to try to think of our writing as a way of digesting the past, then striving to let it go.

But I could see it was too soon for this. We weren't safe enough, established enough. The girls didn't trust themselves, or me, yet.

Ana suggested a letter to themselves now. "Okay, sure, that sounds good," I agreed, glad that this usually taciturn young woman had decided to suggest something. They all wrote pep-rally type pieces. Ana's was all about the drugs that had overtaken her young life. She wanted to save it for "clinical," she told me. "Clinical" was their lingo for therapy sessions, I was yet to learn.

Lori came in; she'd wanted us to end at 4:30 today for some reason. The girls clammed up immediately when she arrived. I saw that they'd already become protective of this space we'd carved from their programmatic days, and cohered as a group more than I'd thought.

I was falling in love with these girls. Despite their painful stories, or maybe because of them, my heart was loosening. I felt as though I was coming out of a long hibernation, opening a door to light I hadn't seen in a very long while.

Nothing Left to Lose

At our next session, again on the sun porch, there was an additional staff person accompanying Ana. The staff member informed me she had to be an arm's length away from Ana at all times. I wondered why, but didn't ask, thinking I would check with Lori later, and not wanting to embarrass Ana. She looked miserable and wrote nothing, but just shifted back and forth on her chair, her overlarge yellow parka making rustling sounds, throughout the whole session.

Everyone seemed sad, and there was a chaotic feeling in the air. They were restless, and we got off to a late start. A bunch of rotting pumpkins sat in the middle of the table. They smelled. I wondered why someone hadn't taken them away.

"We never got to eat lunch," Nia spoke up.

"Sharon, we have to leave early so we can go shopping," Mayra let me know.

"Shopping? Are you going to the mall or something?"

They laughed. "No, to Torrington for groceries, Sharon!"

I could hear the "duh" in their voices. I wondered why they would embrace this boring task, but I guessed that going off grounds anywhere was a strange kind of treat when one was "locked up," as they constantly declared they were at Touchstone.

As it turned out, they didn't get to go after all, but were told they had to go to "drill." It all seemed so militaristic here. The girls always counted off when they lined up for what was called "transition" and walked places in straight lines like I'd had to in Catholic school.

I had so much more to learn about this place and its operation, their proclivities, capacities. They didn't get the poem I read today, about a woman who was being attacked. I'd wanted them to write in the persona of the woman, thinking they could relate. No, too soon for this, again. They didn't want to, nor did they want to write about "a time I was happy."

"We're never happy, Sharon," Nia told me.

Instead La Toya wrote about lovemaking with her boyfriend, in great detail, and read it to us with feeling. Kaylee responded, even though we weren't supposed to respond. "I don't think that's good for a virgin's ears to hear." I was impressed that she had enough self-knowledge to know that for herself, though everyone tittered.

I needed to find more material they could relate to. I wanted to have a space we could meet in that was warm and comfortable, where we wouldn't be constantly interrupted. When I got home, I called Lori to ask about this.

"We need a permanent meeting place, one that lets the girls know that Touchstone respects the group," I told her. "And what happened with Ana?"

"Yes, I know. Let's make it the dorm basement; we just put new carpeting down there, is that all right? Ana was expressing suicidal thoughts, so we had to put her on a 'tight.' She'll be watched for twenty-four hours until we think she's okay. You're going to keep coming, aren't you, Sharon?"

"Oh yes, Lori. Poor Ana. That is awful. I am so sorry."

"Well, that's what happens around here."

And yes, as I was to find out in the upcoming years, it surely was. Fights, restraints, actual suicide attempts, refusals to participate in the program or go to school, throwing chairs, assaulting staff members, contraband smuggling, cops on campus. Touchstone was a tough environment, a rough place to be for both girls and staff.

But it was alive and spirited, as my existence had not been. Their energy was bringing me to life again, and I wanted more than ever for the world at large to hear their voices, know their stories, what caused them to act out in such rebellious ways.

* * *

Puzzled friends, relatives, and colleagues, asked me constantly why I wanted to do this work—what could be in it for me? And wouldn't it take away valuable time from my own writing? And how about my therapy practice?

I struggled to answer, finally developing a response convincing enough to satisfy them. I said I'd felt I'd lived much of my own life imprisoned— in the deadened world of the forties and fifties, a world in which everything was prescribed—our clothing, our thoughts, our choices. Women had few options but serving men and children as wives and mothers in capacities that had been determined by thousands of years of social programming. Children, especially girls, were to be "seen and not heard." And in the church that ruled my life along with my parents, women had seemed even more servile than my mother, as nuns ironing the elaborate priestly garments, dusting the altars, teaching in parochial schools headed by priests.

My husband John and I had married young, in 1964, right after college. I'd worked for a short time as a teacher, but then chose to stay home to care for our much-loved but unplanned children while my husband freely pursued his medical career. He and I had been deeply in love, total equals when we married, but as husband and wife, the new roles we'd been forced to inhabit, balance in our young relationship was quickly destroyed.

At times, it felt like a locked box with no key I could find.

The therapy that I had both received and practiced over the years seemed limiting, after my son Geoff's death. Many of the people who came to me for help were reluctant to do the real work of change; they wanted out of their pain with as little effort as possible. I understood, I loved them, we worked hard together, but it was tough going, especially with my new perspective.

I needed work I could believe in more.

The Buddhist Vipassana mindfulness practice I had begun seven years earlier on a meditation retreat in New Mexico was pushing me to try to discover a new way of living and working. The "Four Noble Truths" of the Buddhist dharma resonated more powerfully with me than the psychological concepts I had long used as guideposts for my life.

The first noble truth informs us that suffering is an unavoidable fact of human existence, and that there are varieties of suffering—the kind that comes from outside, and the kind that we create ourselves. The second states that suffering is caused by craving, wanting things to be other than they are. The third tells us that there is a way to end suffering. And the fourth is the "how-to" —that elusive and powerful summons to let go of that suffering through the "noble eightfold path." Mindfulness meditation was one of its most useful tools, and I'd been attempting to practice it for years since my first retreat, sitting cross-legged on my cushion for a half hour each day, watching my thoughts rise and fall and rise again.

But those thoughts had been mostly filled with anguish about my dead son, and desire to have him returned to me.

Craving. I couldn't get away from it.

The Buddha's noble truths were pragmatic, and held the seeds of freedom, though I was far from being able to truly live them. "Letting go"—what did that really mean? I still needed my grief, and was reluctant to be without it. I couldn't yet grasp how accepting things as they are wholeheartedly was the key to balance and peace, though that was the continual message of the many retreats I'd been on.

And I definitely couldn't see how accepting things as they were with Touchstone and the girls could be liberating; to me that seemed like giving up. But I was determined to persevere, knowing, at some deeper level, that this acceptance was something I *had* to learn.

And I'd always lived by "Think not what your country can do for you, but what you can do for your country," as President Kennedy had exhorted us all in the tumultuous sixties. I'd been a college student in Washington , DC, both when he'd been inaugurated and when he'd been assassinated, and the words ran deep for me.

But what blasted all these predictable responses out of the water was this: somehow, somewhere in my unconscious, I'd known I needed these girls as teachers. I hadn't known how or where to find them until now. My white privilege and life experience was so limiting; I was so frozen in pain, so in need of what they had to give me. Sometimes, they seemed more like adults than I did. They knew how to risk, how to stretch themselves despite the monstrous injury done to them, as I seemed not to. They knew how to protect themselves from too much hope. Suffering didn't shock them as it had me; they knew it was simply a fact of their lives. They got all the Buddhist stuff even though they had no knowledge of its heavy rhetoric. I could see that clearly even in the few weeks we'd been together.

"Freedom's just another word for nothing left to lose," sang the Janis Joplin of my young adult days, intoxicating words that had lodged themselves within me, but that I wasn't certain I'd been able to live. I wasn't sure what freedom was exactly; telling the truth of my life in my poems and living with the risk of the telling was the closest I had come to a definition.

I had lost everything with Geoff's death, so yes, I had nothing left to lose.

Was that a kind of freedom, the freedom of total emptiness?

Tricky Business

"You are so nice to bring us all this!" Kaylee said, hugging me. "A whole pack of pens! And candy too."

"Sharon, I'm leaving next week," La Toya told me. I'd known she was close to discharge, but I was distressed when she told me it was really happening. Despite the newness of our relationship, I was already attached. And I would miss her calm presence in the group. She had been a real stabilizer in a sea of unsettledness.

"You are so mature, La Toya, beautiful and smart. Please keep writing. You are talented. Good luck with going home," I said as I hugged her. She beamed.

"Maybe I'll stay until after creative writing," she said.

"So what do you all think about inviting new members into the group?" I asked the room at large.

Brisa, who almost never spoke or wrote anything, said it would be hard to let new girls in when everyone had shared themselves so deeply, and pulled her sweatshirt hood down even further over her face.

"You should only bring in one new girl at a time," said La Toya." Just one to replace me, and then one more when Kaylee leaves."

Ana sucked her thumb and said she didn't care. Nia and Kaylee said they liked the group just the way it was.

"I'll think about it and decide, but I'd like to bring at least one new girl in. We need to give some of the others this opportunity. And all this coming and going will be happening a lot as time goes on."

"We are the ones who should be able to decide, Sharon. It's our group and we want to keep it this way." There was never any problem about knowing just where Nia stood.

"I don't know how we can do that, if people keep leaving," I mused. The makeup of the group and feelings about it were going to be a real issue,

I could see that. This collection of girls had bonded strongly in such a short time.

I *did* want them to make the choice, for us to be a little democratic boat in the sea of Touchstone's prescriptive environment. I hated telling them what to do. But that particular freedom just didn't work in our group. I had to take charge, but I resisted.

I didn't want to be seen as an authoritarian parent figure, like everyone in my past. As a parent myself, I'd swung between wanting to be a friend to my kids and being strict with them, sometimes in the middle, never sure of the right balance.

I'd made so many mistakes. Much of my suffering over Geoff's death was regret over those mistakes and my many flaws.

When my husband and I had traveled with him in Italy the three weeks before he died, we had not been in a great place with each other. After realizing early that traditional marital roles were boxing us in, we determined that both of us needed more space and choice than those constricted roles allowed for. Negotiating that space and choice often created more conflict and stress than there would have been if our marriage was the conventional kind. Those stresses had blossomed more fully when the kids had left home and I began my new work as a family therapist.

I had feared our rocky marital ground was hard to hide, though being with our son who had grown up so much since he'd left us was an incredible tonic for us both.

And his center had shifted away from us. "My life is with my friends now," he'd asserted. It had been a tricky business, navigating this whole new place we were in together. He'd morphed from the short, chubby, naïve boy who'd left home into a slim, tall, and handsome young man with a life in a foreign country. An adult. He was leading us around, speaking a language we didn't know, making decisions about where we'd stay, what we should eat. We just paid the bills, awed by his transformation.

I was hungry to know who he was now, but trying to be careful not to be too intrusive, an attempt at which I generally wasn't very successful. I wanted to know if he had a girlfriend (he did), what his studies were like, his teachers, what he did every day, what he felt about living abroad. We noticed his wheezing, his constant use of his inhaler. The air in Italy was thick, polluted with constant exhaust fumes from the ubiquitous motor scooters. Everyone, it seemed, smoked. We'd suspected how bad it would be, but knew too that we couldn't say no to his dream of a year in Rome.

"I'm handling it, Mom, Dad," he'd say when we asked him about how his asthma had been since he'd left.

I should have pushed more. I should have been able to protect him. That feeling has never completely left me. I didn't know then that most parents who have lost a child struggled with this guilt. That they felt that somehow, if only they had been better parents and people, done something different, anything at all, the child might still be alive— no matter how irrational that concept in the face of reality.

My husband tried to comfort me by repeating over and over that Geoff's death was a random event, that bad things happened all the time with no discernible explanations. I wanted to believe him and I tried, but it was too hard, even with the Buddhist teachings I was struggling to absorb. His words didn't alter my grief, but they eventually contributed to helping me carry it differently.

The autopsy stated that an asthma attack had probably precipitated the fall. An investigation had declared his death an accident, but without a convincing explanation. The Embassy had ruled out foul play as a cause of death, but we never did. There had been a friend with him that night who, we felt, knew something he wasn't telling us.

There were just too many unanswered questions.

We Keep Going

I'd decided to leave the discussion about new members off to the side for now, sure that whatever we decided on today would change or be forgotten the next week.

"Let's get to our prompt for this afternoon, 'Everything I know about fathers.'"

Brisa immediately started to cry. Kaylee pulled me over and whispered that Brisa's father had died recently, and that she didn't want to hear anyone writing bad about their fathers because she didn't have one. I was put into another quandary; should I change for her, be protective, or go ahead and risk it, knowing that they would probably write what they wanted to anyway?

We got into a spirited discussion about possible alternative writing topics; they all wanted to write about boyfriends, sex, love, and hormones.

"Is young love possible?" Kaylee suggested. "A healthy sex life," was Nia's proposal.

I don't have many of the pieces they wrote from that time because I hadn't yet begun typing them up; that happened later on. But when we did write about fathers, Nia told us her father, or the man she'd thought was her father, a drug and alcohol addict, had died when she was six. Turns out her "real" father had disappeared and this one was just someone her mother was "doing the nasty" with. Two deaths, really.

La Toya, whose hair was dyed red this week, wouldn't read her piece because she didn't want to upset Brisa; Brisa read nothing, trying to nestle into the hard blue couch cushions. Kaylee wrote of her love for her father and wish to discuss deeper things with him, then veered off into her anxiety about going home and how she cried herself to sleep every night worrying about how it would be.

"I will be like a new baby being born," she said.

Yes, Kaylee, you will, I thought.

Despite their anger at being locked up and watched all the time, the girls had felt safe here, developed close and important alliances and relationships, and would have to go back to their unsafe homes and neighborhoods, be tempted by their old habits.

Striving to join them with the truth of my own experience, I wrote about my father.

> My father...is Italian and was so overprotective of my sisters and me when I was young that I could hardly do anything. I had to ask permission for every little thing. I couldn't ride a bike because it was too dangerous and wasn't allowed to learn to drive until I was nineteen. I wasn't permitted to go out with a boy until I was sixteen, and then had to be driven by an adult. My parents had to meet and approve of the boy. I couldn't wear lipstick or shave my legs until I was sixteen either, so I sneaked both before.
>
> My father was brought up in tough areas when he was young. He lived in Hell's Kitchen in NYC and in a dicey neighborhood in New Haven until his father was able to get a small grocery store over which they lived, on the corner of Webster and Ashmun Avenues. He told me just recently that he'd been a member of a gang and one night they'd been going to rob a safe. His father wouldn't let him go out that night and the other boys got caught. They were bigger and older than he was and probably would have made him take the blame.
>
> He was a scrappy short kid, always very good-looking, always ready for a fight. His mother loved him with a large and generous love, but his father was cruel and strict, often giving him beatings. He dropped out of school in seventh grade; his teacher walked miles to his house to beg his parents to make him stay in, but it did no good. He was stubborn and wanted what he wanted, to get a job to earn money to buy a car, nice clothes, to run with the gang even though his father made him work in the store. I think he was strict with his daughters because he wanted to protect us from the dangerous world and tough angry boys like he had been.
>
> My father was never around that much when I was growing up and it made me sad and angry.

Part of my developing strategy was to be open and vulnerable in my own writing to encourage them to do the same, and to share parts of my life that might resonate with theirs. My father's story certainly did, as did many aspects of my own.

Our unfolding similarities had me hooked.

And I wasn't giving up on any of them. Who knew when the breakthroughs would come? I just had to keep showing up, right? I had a mission, now, a purpose.

Their pain was pushing mine into a corner.

． ． ．

The girls really seemed to love it when I read to them.

"That gives me hope, Sharon," La Toya said in response to the story I offered at our next meeting from *Sugar In the Raw*, an anthology of young black female teenagers' experiences that focused on race.

"It helps, 'cause I'm leaving tomorrow," La Toya added, fluffing up her latest hairdo.

Mayra seemed to be spiraling into deeper distress. She'd gotten a pass to go home over the weekend, but it turned out that the mother she so adored had gone to Puerto Rico and hadn't even told her she was going. Mayra was furious and heartbroken.

"Maybe I should just get an apartment for independent living instead of trying to go home," she said to me, her dark eyes hooded with confusion and sadness.

"Can you do that? I mean, are you old enough?"

"Yes, Sharon. But I will kill myself if anything happens to my mother."

"You mean you'll feel really sad, maybe like not wanting to live."

"No, I'll kill myself."

Kaylee wrote about how no one understood or could hear her and it would be easier to be under the ground.

"I couldn't read my first piece because everyone would be on top of me."

"What do you mean, Kaylee?"

She just kept repeating that. Finally La Toya said they'd just do "a tight" on her. So I guessed she had suicidal ideation, or maybe was really suicidal. She and La Toya were terrified of going home, of what unknown waited there.

Or maybe a formerly fearsome known.

Nia wrote her opinion of a healthy sex life: if you sleep with someone you should love that person.

Okay, I thought, *that's good.*

La Toya had had a biopsy done on nodes under her arm. While the other girls were threatening to kill themselves, she was worried about dying. Her aunt had had breast cancer at sixteen, she said, and her grandmother has it too, she told me, serious and scared. And La Toya was in a gang, so she'd have to deal with that pressure when she got home.

I was overwhelmed again. Nothing I had ever known or experienced had prepared me for these discussions, these litanies of anguish. There were no more easy solutions here than there had been for my son's death, any more than there were for me.

A staff member came in with the new girl, Tiffany. Despite the resistance they'd voiced before, to my surprise, no one protested. Tiffany was arresting, a flawless caramel color with jet-black hair gelled into ringlets and a fierce anger I could see even from a distance, like steam rising.

The group was changing already, and it seemed that we'd only just found stable ground.

I felt scared and dumb. Every week I was faced with something I'd not been able to anticipate and plan for.

At a time when it would have been helpful to remember those four noble truths of the Buddha and the insight they offered, I panicked, worried that Tiffany would unbalance the group and that the old girls would reject her.

I had no control, none at all.

Taos

Seven years before starting my program at Touchstone, I visited Taos, New Mexico, for a workshop with Natalie Goldberg, a writing guru from whom I have learned so much that helped me in the writing groups I'd led for women, and now these at Touchstone. There I met Clara Rosemarda, a psychic, who offered to give us "readings."

At that time, only five years after Geoff had died, I was mired in a cavernous hole of anguish, with no clue as to how to climb out. Skeptical, cynical, I refused to consider having a reading until it was almost time to leave. But, desperate with distress, I reluctantly decided to give her a try. After all, I had come all the way to New Mexico, the land of free spirits, alternative lifestyles, and curative mineral springs, in search of something. Maybe this reading could be the succor I'd sought.

I don't remember much of what Clara said except that I was in a very dark place, and that I needed to meditate.

Meditate! I wanted no part of that, imagining a roomful of white robed devotees bowing to a guru-master, male, probably, like the guru Maharaj-Ji my brothers-in-law had worshipped. My long Catholic experience with empty rituals had soured me on anything that had even a faint scent of religion.

I'd left that Catholic church in 1970, but when we'd needed to bury Geoff, we'd chosen a Catholic cemetery. In order to do this, we'd been required to have a priest be co-celebrant at the memorial service held in the Congregational church, presided over by a caring minister with whom I'd worked at the local mental health center.

We asked my husband's father's cousin, a monsignor who had married us, and he'd refused, saying he had prior plans, presiding at a communion, I think. His own cousin's grandson! But I knew the reason for his demurral was the non-Catholic service.

Fortunately, friends scrambled and found us a more broadminded and humane priest. This experience, along with countless others, had only cemented the certainty that I was right in my decision to erase religion from my life. But I'd been left with an echoing hollow where God and prayer had been, at a time in my life when something spiritual might have been a useful life jacket.

"Sharon, how'd it go with Clara?" my friend Polly asked after the reading.

"Oh, okay, I guess. Interesting. She told me I should meditate." I didn't know that Polly had a long practice of mindfulness meditation and had lived with her family for years at the Lama Foundation, a spiritual community in the Sangre De Cristo mountains, seventeen miles north of Taos.

"Well? Are you going to?"

"No way." Actually, I had no real idea what meditation was, or what it would have entailed, but then I was determined to keep believing that nothing could help me. I was caught in grief like a mouse in one of those sticky traps, still alive, but unable to move forward or get free. And I wasn't sure I wanted to get free. To do so would have felt like a betrayal of my love for my son.

"Look, Sharon, there's a retreat coming up this summer at Lama Foundation. It's ten days, and Joseph Goldstein and Sharon Salzburg are leading it. They are fantastic. You have to come." (Joseph and Sharon are two of the preeminent Western meditation teachers of our time).

"No way, Polly. I can't. I don't want to, anyway. I told you, it's not for me."

"You can stay at my house before and after. I'm going, and you can come with me. It will change your life. Sharon, you *have* to do this."

Polly was a determined woman. It was almost impossible to say no to her. In the end, I couldn't. I went to the retreat, and she was right, it did change my life. I ate big bowls of hot oats on brisk mountain-cold mornings, showered communally with women in the warm midday sun, sat for hours in the deep peace of the adobe meditation hall. I slept in a rustic cabin with three other women, who told me after the retreat was over that I had cried in my sleep every night.

I'd inhaled that deep silence and the Buddhist dharma like a starving child. The very atmosphere was suffused with a kindness I hadn't known I'd needed so profoundly. I went back to Connecticut incandescent, touched with light in places scarred by my rigid religious past, my son's death, my abusive girlhood.

And I continued my practice by "sitting" many more retreats—at Insight Meditation Society in Barre, Massachusetts; Cambridge Insight Meditation Center; Gaia House near Totnes, in Devon, England; at a boy scout camp in Hawaii; I did a seven-day training for health professionals with Jon Kabat-Zin and Saki Santorelli and sat with Thich Nhat Hanh at Omega Institute in Rhinebeck, New York. I've done years of yoga training, extensive reading on Buddhism, and further education in mindfulness practice and psychotherapy.

Now, I could not imagine life without all of that.

I sat cross-legged on a cushion most days, as I had been taught, paying careful attention to what transpired in my mind as I breathed in, breathed out. Joseph and Sharon had instructed us in how to "note" our thoughts—fantasy, desire, planning, aversion, remembering, restlessness, greed, doubt, clinging, grasping, dwelling. The idea was, in short, that real awareness of what was in our minds would lead to wisdom, helping us to relinquish our attachments and thus lessen our suffering. All in life was imperfect and incomplete, because our world was subject to impermanence. Happy moments pass by, as do sad ones, as will we.

A more lofty aspiration, enlightenment, achieved by long and devoted practice, a far-off goal that I never even contemplated, was the nirvana of no-self. "Aim for the North Star," the Vietnamese monk Thich Nhat Hanh had once said, and I'd thought that was enough for me right now.

But my mind was full of clinging and dwelling, fantasy and desire, aversion and memory. I wanted Geoff back, and couldn't stop hanging on to how much; I was furious at his death, its complete unfairness, and the terrible disruption in my life it had caused. I fantasized constantly about his fall, falling with him, about his dying alone in the night. I imagined him crying out in fear and anguish for me and his father, for his friends, to save him, feeling continual torment that I hadn't been able to. I'd tried to open to these thoughts, acknowledge them, and then let go, over and over again, teaching my mind to carve new neuronal pathways. It was hard going. It still is.

But after being at Touchstone all these months, I began to notice that my thoughts had shifted. Now my mind was full of the girls, their faces, their stories, their traumas, their voices. Geoff continued to be a visitor, but not the constant presence he had been. My mind was possessed by a new object.

I had fallen in love with a group of young women society labeled "delinquent."

Geoff

"How old are you, Sharon?" Mayra wanted to know toward the end of our next meeting.

All the girls had been able to come this afternoon, a few weeks after Tiffany had joined. We were meeting in the dorm basement now, and the regular space was helping with the group's stability. There were fifteen minutes before our time was up; not enough to write another piece, but time to talk.

"I'm fifty-seven."

"Do you have kids?" Brisa asked.

"Yes, I do. One son living, and one who died."

Their questions poured out. "How do you feel? How did it happen? Did you save his clothes? Keep his room?" They wanted me to tell them if he had he been a virgin, had a girlfriend, a baby. Was he on drugs? Was he shot? What had I put into his casket with him? What was his funeral song? Would I sing it?

We'd had "Blowin' in the Wind" played at his funeral, I told them. Music that sang of no answers. The only Bob Dylan they'd heard of was from the movie *Forrest Gump*.

The staff member there today was getting concerned. "Do you want to talk about this?" she asked.

"Of course," I said. "It's okay, really. It's not a problem." Brisa's face was riveted on me. They were all rapt.

"Here's what happened," I said. "He was twenty-one, on his junior year abroad in college, living and studying in Rome. It was the night before his last exam, and he went out to dinner with a friend and then to a pub afterwards. But he didn't stay at the pub, he got up and left and never came back, without telling his friend where he was going. The friend stayed there drinking beer with an American girl. We think Geoff—that's my son's name—was having an asthma attack and went to look for the backpack he'd left at the restaurant they'd been at. His inhaler was in it."

They all nodded. Many of them had asthma and knew what an inhaler was.

"So what happened was that he fell off a very high wall along the Tiber River—fifty feet high. No one saw him, it was late at night. We think he'd been heading back to the dorm, or maybe to his apartment, and just couldn't go on because of the wheezing, stopped to lie down or sit on the wall, and then he fell, somehow. He had a branch in his hand, he must have grabbed it knowing he was falling." This is the place I can never get beyond in the telling without tears. "The police found him the next morning."

"Aww, Sharon." Kaylee, who hadn't left yet despite her avowals that she'd be gone when I returned the following week, came up and put her arm around me.

"Don't you wish you had a daughter?" she asked.

"Oh yes," I said. "I do. But now I have all of you."

They laughed and smiled. "How do you stand it?" someone else asked.

"I'm like you," I said. "I try to work at getting past the hard place, the place that hurts and keeps me stuck—but there's a place in me, a hole, what had been there gone forever. I'll never be the same again." I could see Brisa nodding in understanding. Maybe she'd read to us next week.

"And I write, a lot, and it really helps, and that's why I want you to write too. We all have important stories to tell. And now it's time to go for today. Thanks for asking about Geoff, and for caring. You can ask me anything, anytime."

They looked solemn as they lined up for transition. There was none of the usual pushing and jostling and complaining. I'd told that story so many times, but somehow this time was different. It had felt like they'd really wanted to know about Geoff in a way others usually did not. Most people asked to be polite, out of curiosity, or because it was the right thing to do. Sometimes they backed away, looked down, or changed the subject. They dreaded the emotion that might come up in me, or themselves.

But, as I gave the answers to the girls' questions, I sensed bridges of shared pain building between us. It was almost like all we'd lost was in the room with us, aching and breathing, a big beating pulse of abuse and betrayals, deaths and assorted other wounds, a presence we had to honor in a new way, with each other.

Maybe, I thought, maybe I'm not so alone. Maybe Geoff has led me here, to these strong, beautiful, real young women, to comfort me, to steer me away from my grief over his absence and push me into the hearts of others.

On the ride home that thought kept coming up—as it would for years.

Christmas

It upset everyone in my families that I couldn't be happier at this time of year. Geoff's birthday was December 1, and that began the season of escalating heartache for me. He'd always loved the holidays so, had been the one of my two sons to most want to help make and decorate Christmas cookies, hang ornaments on the tree as we reminisced about each one, make fancy place cards for our Christmas dinner. The buying of presents had been an earnest task for him, requiring long contemplation over each choice. He'd always saved his money to buy gifts for each of us, and my parents, as well as others who were special in his life.

The Christmas before he'd died, he'd been in Rome, and had stayed on in Europe to travel with his college friends, since he was continuing in the program for the second semester. He'd had to move out of the dorm and into a cheap *pensione* before they arrived.

How I'd felt his loneliness when he called from a pay phone near the Vatican on Christmas Eve.

"It's pouring here," he'd said over the static on the line. "How's Sasha?" (our black Lab).

I knew he'd never let us know that he wished he were home at Christmas and not by himself in the cold rain. He'd gone to the Amalfi Coast with one friend already, and now would travel to Lugano, Lucerne, and Munich for New Year's Eve, and to Yugoslavia for skiing with two more friends.

I was thrilled that he had these great opportunities. I asked him about the trips and he sketched some of the details for us, said how grateful he'd been to have the money to make them.

I was grateful too. The money had been challenging to scrape up, but we'd managed to supplement what we could afford with appreciated contributions from both of my parents.

Later, I imagined the excruciating regrets I would have suffered had we not had it to give.

The spring of his sophomore year, when he'd called one afternoon from school to tell me he'd gotten into the Trinity College program, the only one that offered the full year abroad in Rome that he badly wanted, I began to cry.

"Mom," he scolded, "why are you crying? This is the happiest day of my life."

Because it was 1986. Terrorists had put bombs in the Fiumicino airport, and some had gone off. Because he had asthma and the air in Rome was toxic.

"Because I'm so afraid something is going to happen to you," I'd said to him.

* * *

I had struggled over gifts for the girls. What to get, what would they like, how much should I spend? It didn't seem right to make a big splash with fancy presents, and I knew I couldn't pick out individual gifts for each. That would never have worked, probably would have fed jealousies and started fights. So I settled on some rhinestone hair ornaments, each one different, that I'd seen on a trip to the Gap. Because the price tags were gummed on so hard, I'd had a really hard time scraping them off, so they ended up seeing what I'd paid.

"You spent $5.98 on me?" said Brisa, shocked. "I'd never do that for anyone."

"I feel special," said Nia, dancing around the room.

Kaylee went into the bathroom to put the clip in her hair, came out to show me with that beautiful half-smile of hers. I would miss her so much.

I handed back their typed pieces; Nia was the only one happy with hers. Before the meeting, I'd spoken to the assistant director about Brisa and Ana—Brisa sleeping all the time, Ana not writing anything. Brisa sat straight up throughout our session today and volunteered to read her work twice. Ana didn't read, but promised she would next time. Tiffany had a doctor's appointment, so wasn't with us, but I gave her gift to Kaylee to give to her.

I asked the girls to write about Christmas. That was a big mistake. They all wrote unconvincing sentimental pieces, imagining Hallmark holidays with their families that probably would never happen.

They just weren't into it today, talking with each other, ignoring me. I gave them "home" as the next prompt.

> My red farmhouse is home. I'll drive up the gravel driveway tonight and see the candles lit in all its windows and feel its welcome. Being here with you girls makes me appreciate home. That I have a choice to go home when I want to, that I have a home to go to. After my son died, the cemetery was home. I went there every day and cried, sat by his gravestone trying to make myself believe he was really dead. I wanted to be there more than anywhere else, the house I lived in then didn't feel like home anymore. I'd bring rocks from the beach and planted flowers there. Sometimes my husband and I would just go and sit. We felt like we were with him then.

Maybe that had been too sad for today? I felt so unsure about what I was doing here when the girls were unresponsive like this. I'd asked them to write a goodbye to Kaylee, another grave miscalculation.

"We don't care about her, so there's nothing to write," Nia had said. The others, silent, seemed to agree. Kaylee, glaring, crumpled her piece, throwing it on the floor.

I drove back to Lakeville through a snowstorm on slippery, treacherous roads. How inviting those window candles looked when I came up my driveway, the Christmas tree splendid with lights and all our old ornaments hanging on the fresh green boughs. Home. Cozy, warm—what a counterpoint to Touchstone's dreariness and the sullenness of the girls that afternoon. Maybe Christmas wouldn't feel so bad this year.

Gratitude, so long a stranger in my life, filled me as I walked into the kitchen and hugged my surprised husband hard.

I Am Not a Juvenile Delinquent

At our first meeting of the new year, I'd announced with what I hoped was ringing resolve, "Girls, I want to make a fresh start for this new year. I still really want to help you all tell your important stories, but I'm thinking of coming only every other week. You've been disrespectful a lot, and some of you don't participate at all. It makes me wonder if you really want to do this poetry group."

The girls didn't respond with reassurance, just looked blank and sad.

Angel, the staff person assigned to the group that day, spent the session riding the exercise bike that usually sat unused in the back of the dorm basement.

At least Mayra had moved the couches and chairs into a circle without being asked, and was pleased to see her piece typed up. Brisa looked awake for once, but Ana's eyes were already closing. Nia was stretched out on another couch. Kaylee had finally left and taken with her the infectious liveliness she'd brought to the group.

"Please, girls, focus up! I am speaking to you. And sit up, Nia and Ana. We are going to work on group poems today, but first we'll try 'I remember.' Just write about the first thing that comes to your mind when you think that phrase, okay?"

During this write, Ana continued to sleep. Nia confronted her, said she wasn't showing respect for any of us. Ana got up and went to Angel for support.

"Ana, you are free to leave the group if that's what you choose, but I hope you will stay for the rest of today."

"I need to leave, Sharon." She went to call someone on the phone. Angel was talking out loud on his walkie-talkie while we were writing.

"Angel, could you please be quiet?" I said. "You are not showing respect for us."

They both left and Lesley, a young, enthusiastic staff person who was a much better fit for the group, came in while Mayra was reading. Nia was laughing and Lesley asked her to stop, saying it was not respectful, that it could hurt others' feelings.

"But what she wrote is funny, Lesley! That's why I'm laughing."

We are all relieved that Ana is gone, I thought. She'd never really wanted to be here. I'd talk with her after the session was over.

"Okay, I'm going to read you this poem a group of girls at the Los Angeles detention center wrote that was published in *Teen Voices*, the magazine I brought in last week. It's called *I Am Not a Juvenile Delinquent*. I want each of you to call out a phrase like the ones in the poem—tell me who you are, what you're not. Think you can do that?"

Ideas came pouring out and I wrote them down as fast as I could. They really got it, all the counterpoints, the shadow selves, the mixture of good and bad, and how real it made the title. And Brisa was really involved.

I Am Not a Juvenile Delinquent

I am a black queen
I am a unique individual
I am a woman of feeling
I am an understandable outspoken queen
I am a woman of passion born of desperation
I am a drug addict
I am a fiend
I am a loving person, I shine
I show no mercy
I am a firebug with a beautiful light that burns to the touch
I am a menace to society
I am a name brand
I represent pure beauty
I am the fifth element
I am tension
My name is beautiful but I'm filled with rage
I am the pregnant virgin
I am dead
I am the fire, touch me, you will burn
I am the foundation of this creed

I Am Not a Juvenile Delinquent

I have no faith
I am Athena
I am Scorpio
I am Leo
I am Aquarius
I am you
I am me
We are society
We are the millennium
We are the future
We can make it better
We are life

"This is so good, girls. This is fantastic!! What a great job you've done."
I was almost flying. All the girls had participated excitedly, willingly,
eagerly. *Maybe I'd been too hard on them earlier?* I thought. *Maybe their
bad behavior was really my fault, not having prompts catchy enough to hold
their attention?*

Everyone's mood had shifted. I was so buzzed by the powerful poem
and their excited participation that I just wanted to keep going, ride the
creative wind that had suddenly whipped up in the dorm basement. I
wished so much that Kaylee had still been there. She would have loved it
and would have had some great lines to throw into the mix.

I couldn't let her go, yet.

"Let's try another group poem," I said, wanting to move fast, build on
success. "How about 'what mama said'?" They warmed to that quickly
and threw out ideas faster than I could write them down. I had to get
them to stop and repeat several times.

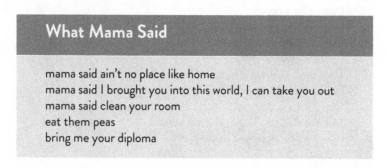

What Mama Said

mama said ain't no place like home
mama said I brought you into this world, I can take you out
mama said clean your room
eat them peas
bring me your diploma

don't get that best Sunday outfit dirty
come home before the streetlights come on
say that again and I'll smack your face out
keep cryin' and I'll give you something to cry about
don't let nobody play in your hair
don't come home from school dirty 'cause we goin' some-
where
mama said I love you
no matter how old you are you're still going to be my baby
girl
go to the bathroom before you go to bed
don't let nobody fool you, girl
if somebody hits you, hit them back
never perm your hair
if you hit me you better run
always try
if you go to school and graduate I'll buy you a car
I'll always be there for you
don't answer on my phone when I'm not home
go to the store with the food stamps, buy some bread, some
milk, some eggs
come straight home from school
if my door closed, always knock
don't talk back
never talk to strangers
open the door for no one
watch yo' mouth, girl

"Sharon, that was fun!" Nia said. Lesley, the new staff support person, came up and told me how terrific she thought the session had been.

"If I can work it out," she said, "do you think I could come and be the staff for this group every week?"

"Lesley, how excellent that would be! Do you really think you could make that happen?"

"Well, I think I can. I want to. I'll try."

The girls hugged me as they left with her. Physical contact, a "boundary violation," was strictly forbidden between the girls and their peers as well as staff, but that was another expectation that we'd relaxed in our group. Lesley did not comment, but joined in the hugging, a good sign.

No one ever told me I had to stop allowing hugs. They just became an accepted part of poetry group, along with the allowance for slang and expletives and the excusal from the normative expectations like facials and confrontations.

In any case, despite the fact that I thought the boundary violation rule necessary in the larger community for the safety of the girls—many of whom had experienced severe trauma due to such violation—the girls were hungry for hugs. Our space was clearly safe, and they often seemed like the perfect and needed finish to our meetings, a way to say goodbye, an affirmation of them and their stories.

• • •

I had to go to the house and see Ana. She looked so dejected, her hair clumped with gel, a yellowish stain on her blue sweatshirt. We spent forty-five minutes talking.

"Sharon, I was at my limit, ready to cry. Writing is not my hobby, but I wanted to try. I never really felt safe in the group—I'm just too sensitive."

"Well, I sure wish you'd talked to me about this long ago. I guess I should have brought it up earlier, but there was always so much going on. And yes, there are many differences in personality and style with you and the others, that's true, but that's true in life out in the real world, too."

"It was hard for me to hear them using slang and talking about drugs."

She stopped for a minute, looking down. "Drugs and alcohol were my big problems before I got here. And I'm tired from all the work in the kitchen"—at that time all the girls had daily housekeeping jobs assigned to them—"and being on Level 3," she said proudly. "I'm higher than all the others."

After our conversation, I felt okay about letting her leave, though I was angry with myself for allowing the decision to be delayed for so long. I hadn't wanted to admit defeat. The girls were teaching me again, that I needed to do a better job of accepting the way things are, that impermanence and difficulties are just part of life, especially at Touchstone.

I knew I needed to make "this is the way it is right now" my daily mantra, but the faith it took to really believe that hadn't yet made it into my neuronal programming.

Sister Benedicta

Finally, I was starting to get it. These girls were *me* as an adolescent, despite the fact that I'd worn the blue uniform of a studious good girl in contrast to their revealing attire, despite the fact that I'd lived in in an affluent suburb instead of the projects of Hartford or Bridgeport. I'd had no idea that the term "youth at risk," if it had even been coined yet, had applied to me. But my mother got angry a lot, hit us often with my father's belt, chain-smoked Phillip Morris cigarettes. My father rarely came home until late at night, and when he was there, he and my mother frequently fought. When he'd bring friends with him, they'd often be drunk. He would become enraged when my mother wisely locked up the liquor cabinet, when a pillow was out of place, a meal not on time, or a couch unsmoothed. He was king of the castle we lived in, he'd built it with money he'd considered his, and our job was to look like a family that belonged there.

I'd been at risk for anger, for depression, for anxiety, for creating unhealthy relationships in adult life, for nicotine and alcohol addiction, for constant feelings of shame. I'd been at risk for crying into my pillow every night, for perfectionism, for the drive to prove that I was okay to my parents, teachers, and friends. And I didn't know that some of those friends, behind the doors of their nice white colonials, were also youth at risk, being yelled at and hit, with brothers in their beds at night, inebriated fathers passed out on couches every day after work, tipsy mothers burning their dinners.

No one ever spoke of such things back then. I don't think there was any Department of Children and Families to call. No one would have called it anyway. Speaking of our problems in confession, or taking the chance to confide in a teacher, were daring gambles. Being told that what was happening in our lives was God's will and that suffering would make us strong were predictable answers that pathetically failed to be of any support to us. We needed so much to learn that we were okay as we were, how to get help to deal with our difficult home situations. We needed confidence and inspiration instead of self-abnegation. We needed to be taught the ability to reflect on our experience.

But we never received those essential lessons.

> "In its glory days, especially in the 1940's and 1950's, the Catholic Church constructed a virtual state-within-a-state so Catholics could live almost their entire lives within a thick cocoon of Catholic institutions."
>
> —**Charles R. Morris**, *American Catholic*

That's the world I'd lived in as a girl. There was church on Sunday, confession on Saturday, catechism classes every week in the church basement. When I was in sixth grade, my parents were told it was a mortal sin not to send your children to Catholic school, and there wasn't one in our town. We weren't going to move, so I was made to travel to a city an hour and a half away by bus to attend St. Joseph Cathedral School.

A mortal sin meant you'd go to hell, that big underground furnace. Medieval notion that it was, people believed it. My parents believed it. I believed it.

At St. Joseph's, there were close to fifty kids in each classroom, most coming from the area around the cathedral. We were taught by nuns in black serge and white starch, long clanking rosaries cinched to their waists with heavy leather straps. The thick heels on their black oxfords made a delicate tapping sound on our school's wide polished floors as they glided, dark angels, from place to place.

My mother drove me, that first day of school, in our coral Cadillac. It was humiliating to have arrived at the large old red-brick building in that garish car, and I got out of it as fast as I could, though unsure what to do or where to go. There seemed to be different entrances for boys and girls, so when I saw the other kids lining up in silence, I quickly fell in with the girls, my stomach burning with agitation.

In silence, we walked into the basement, a grim cave of gray cement. This was where I'd eat my brown-bag lunch every day, sitting at a long barracks-like table with the few other kids that didn't walk home for the hour and a half lunch period. I was scared, everything was so different, but there was a part of me that was exhilarated too, always ready for something unknown that would take me away from my family's painful life.

My new classroom was on the second floor, where the older kids were. Wooden desks were bolted to the scuffed floor. They even had inkwells, which we used for penmanship practice. Uncomfortable bench seats were attached just far enough away from the desks to be a disagreeable stretch.

We marched into this austere and unwelcoming space, girls first, then boys. Sister Benedicta read off our names and we filed into our seats, again, boys on one side, girls on the other.

Sister must have given us some assignment, as I remember her walking slowly up and down the aisles, perhaps to see if everyone was doing what they were supposed to. She was young, with dark brown eyes and pale skin, her face an exquisite portrait framed by a starched and pleated white coif.

She stopped at my desk. My stomach clenched. I was sure I'd done something wrong, already terrified of displeasing my new teacher.

Sister Benedicta placed her hand on the puffy sleeve of my new nylon blouse. "I could put a little mouse in there and watch it run around," she said, meeting my frightened brown eyes with her kind gaze. I think it was from that very moment I was in love. I could tell right away that she saw me, the real Sharon, the Sharon no one else had ever truly seen, not my parents or sisters, not any of my friends or other teachers.

This was the woman who would become my mentor and confidant for the next twenty years. This was the teacher I'd write to and visit as a needy, hurting adolescent looking for guidance, love, and support. This was the nun I'd wanted to follow into the convent, not because I loved God so much, but because I loved her. The two loves were mixed up, tangled and confused.

Sister Benedicta was the person who probably mostly inspired my circuitous pilgrimage to Touchstone. I think I wanted to be to the girls what she hadn't been able to be to me. As a nun, she was choked by the confines of her beliefs and life choices. And we were both rooted in the heavy Catholic culture of the '50s. But the many words she'd written me over the years had connected with the thread of my longings, as well as with my fears. They bit deep into a primitive place inside me, the place that craved love and acceptance. I'd long taken refuge in their unlikely shelter, though in my early adult life I'd easily cast off the Catholic Church with my growing grasp of its profound hypocrisy.

I wrote her often, visited and called her when I could. Sister Benedicta told me that suffering was a mark of God's love. She told me that I was separate from God, and to be close to Him, the only experience that had real meaning in life, there were many tasks I had to perform and keep performing. That if I was not good, I must be bad. That if I was not right, I must be wrong. In this black-and-white soil, the seeds of my often-disabling perfectionism took root and began to flourish.

She told me repeatedly to offer my own will to God, that He would supply what I needed, and when.

But the most troublesome message was this one, written in delicate script, in one of her letters to me at a time in which I was struggling with some adolescent crisis:

> "Most of life's unhappiness that is experienced is because of self before all else...when self should be last, lowest, and least."

I had a hard time feeling confident, empowered, and comforted by these words and ideas, seemingly meant more for someone in a religious order than a teenage girl trying to find out who she was. But because I loved her, I took them in and tried to apply her advice to my life. In the Catholic culture I was suffused in, they made a strange kind of sense.

However, I was already so strict with myself that it made me even more judgmental and self-critical. I couldn't feel good about who I was, who I was becoming. I didn't understand how to interpret God's will. And how would I know what was God's will and not that of my parents or the Church's?

If only I'd had someone like me to talk to back then.

I had a chance to rewrite my history at Touchstone, to be that someone for the girls.

Push

It had been seven months since our first meeting.

"Yay, Sharon! Lori told me I could be the regular staff for the poetry group!"

Lesley, the staff member who'd hoped to accompany me and the group, greeted me at the door with this great information, wearing a pink ball cap and a huge smile.

"Yay, Lesley!" We high-fived each other and went to look for the girls.

Lesley was young, energetic, and open-hearted. She really loved and understood the girls, and they liked her too. She was extremely supportive of this poetry program in a culture that was not. I was sure it would make a huge difference.

Tiffany was still in her room. When she finally joined us, she looked as beautiful as usual today in a red t-shirt, her long hair in ringlets around her troubled face. Long serious about writing, she'd told me she planned to write a book of poems called *The Pregnant Virgin*. She became terribly upset when I told her I knew of a book by the same name.

"No, Sharon, that's *my* title."

"And it's a terrific one, Tiffany, with that obvious contradiction that makes people wake up and think. You are so smart to think of it. But maybe it would be hard to use if there was already another book by that name."

"Will you bring in the book for me to see? Then I'll believe it."

"Okay, sure. Do you have your piece from last time so I can type it?"

"Yeah, it's right here."

We had new girls, Isabella and Nadia, friends of Nia and Mayra who had recommended them. Without further discussion or rebellion, we'd settled into the method that continued to work for the rest of the year—just bringing in other girls who were interested when old ones were discharged.

"Do you know what poetry group is all about?" I asked them.

"Yeah, miss," they told us. "It's about struggling—about expressing yourself."

"Yup, that's right." I went over the expectations again, as a refresher/reminder to everyone.

"Today, I've brought in a book by a woman named Sapphire called *Push*, thought I would start reading it to you; I think you'll connect with the main character, Precious."

The girls were captivated from the very beginning and never wanted me to stop reading. "Keep going," they'd say every time I paused.

> "Well then, Clareece, I'm afraid I'm going to have to suspend you—"
>
> "For what!"
>
> "You're pregnant and—"
>
> "You can't suspend me for being pregnant, I got rights!"
>
> "Your attitude, Clareece, is one of total uncooperation—"
>
> I reached over the desk. I was gonna yank her fat ass out that chair.[1]

"I have to stop so we can write, girls. Write about an experience similar to Precious's, okay?"

Nadia's piece was about being pregnant and thrown out of the house by her mother to live with the baby's father, who didn't even know she was pregnant. She began to cry after reading it, and Nia went over to comfort her. I offered Kleenex and patted her knee, but didn't want to make her feel self-conscious or encourage discussion, so I suggested we keep going. Brisa actually volunteered this time and they all wrote such moving pieces. I was intoxicated by the increasing insight and depth of their writing. They were slowly learning how to reflect on their experience, such an important task for maturation, by creating art from their broken lives in our groups.

---

1   Sapphire, *Push*, pg. 8

"Will you bring in some of your poems, Sharon?" Tiffany asked at the end of the session.

"Yes, we really want to see them. And pictures of your family, your son, especially. We want to see what he looks like," Nia asked.

"I love that book you read to us, Sharon," Nadia said. "Precious could be our friend. Are you going to read more next week?"

Nia chimed in, "I love Precious! They are so mean to her, I want to hug her. You've got to read more to us!"

"Okay, sure I will, next time we meet. And I'll bring pictures and poems too."

I was exhilarated about the resonance Precious and *Push* had had with them. Identifying with her was clearly helping them to feel less alone and more self-aware. I hoped I'd finally hit on something that would sustain their interest—for a few weeks, anyway—and challenge them to go even deeper into their own experiences.

• • •

My life now revolved around this place. Typing up the poems took many hours, as did traveling back and forth to Litchfield, the group itself, and all the phone calls to Lori. But mostly the change was about what took up space in my head.

I thought about the girls and their lives all the time. Their stories crowded my insides, transforming the exhausted mourning that had been living there since Geoff had died. Unexpectedly, my grief was becoming an affirmation, something that matched the size of the vast love I had for him, something that connected me to others rather than isolating me from them.

It was as if the mourning had refreshed the knowledge of why I loved, what my values were. My broken heart was saying a holy yes to these locked-up, struggling, awesome young women. I felt more at home with them than I did with almost anyone else. They told me things about the insides of them that matched the insides of me. I could be a self with them that was not possible in the rest of my life. Clearly, I was in a more powerful position than that of the girls, a privileged adult who was not incarcerated, but we were equals, in the most important ways. We understood suffering. We'd all come from unsafe families. We accepted each other wholly.

And, although I was still working as a family therapist, this Touchstone work felt more vital than my practice, where my clients and I were always in asymmetrical, boundaried roles. That was appropriate and necessary for effective therapy work, but sometimes felt very heavy and lonely to me. I carried my worries and anxieties about my clients home as burdens of responsibility, not like the joy, fascination, and frustration I felt with the girls. And even though I ached with them through their crises, depressions, cutting, and hospitalizations, I knew there were clinicians at Touchstone whose job it was to deal with these situations on a daily basis; it was not my load to carry in that particular way.

Grief still blanketed me, but its cold cover had thawed at Touchstone.

Mother's Day at the Morgue

I was going on a mindfulness retreat and then on to babysit for my new grandson in the next weeks, so I would have missed a whole month had I not shown up tonight. It was 6:30, different from our regular time, but I was certain I needed to drive down, despite the icy January weather.

The girls were still in the dining room, eating and talking, when I arrived.

Slowly, they gathered, and we walked over to the dorm with a male staff member.

We settled into the circle of chairs and couches they pulled together.

"I'm sorry for coming at such an odd time but I wanted to see you before I'd be away for a while," I said, pulling off my boots.

"Well, I have to leave at 7:00, I have church," Mayra informed me.

"Church?" I was confused.

"It's Bible Study," someone told me.

"Will you read *Push* again, Sharon? We want to hear what happens to Precious."

"He's not going to let you," Nia said, pointing to the male staff member with us tonight. "When we were watching that movie about the abused woman in Torrington, he made us stop."

He'd heard us, of course, and offered reassurance. "Don't worry, ladies"—staff always called the girls "ladies"—"I'll be a fly on the wall."

Lesley worked second shift, so she'd already gone home and couldn't be with us tonight.

"Great, thank you, Hiram. Sure, yes of course I'll read from *Push*, but I brought the pictures and the poems you asked for last time. Do you still want to see them?"

They'd forgotten, and I felt a little awkward with my reminder.

"Yes, Sharon! Let's see them!" They all swarmed me.

I passed around the photos.

"Is your husband a doctor?"

"What makes you think that?" I was amazed, because he actually *was* a doctor.

"He just looks like one. And Geoff, that's your dead son, right? He looks like a college boy."

As always, I was taken aback by their insight and interest in my life, but tried to remember always, as I had as a therapist, that what I shared should be for their benefit and not mine.

"So, I'll read you one of my poems, okay?"

Mother's Day at the Morgue

The room smells, phenol fumes,
tobacco smoke. The once-white
walls are grimed, but the sheets
that wrap him are pure as baby
swaddling. I know another mother
has bleached and ironed them for me.
He is under glass, a treasure.
Our hands grasp the hard angles.
I am crooning to my child, my hands
pressing their prints everywhere.
His eyes are closed, he is sleeping
so peacefully. The mothers at this place
of strange caring have washed
his hair, pulled it back from his forehead.
Soon he will wake and walk to me.
I am glad they have covered him.
I do not ask him to open his eyes.
My hands no longer feel glass but
his soft skin, the baby body I was
allowed to touch when he was mine.
I hear sounds in the room. Perhaps
they are coming from outside? Someone
is screaming. My baby, my child. I try
to climb on the box. The men are kind

Mother's Day at the Morgue

> they hold my hands. I want to hit them.
> The room is hot and the doctors come
> at us smoking their cigarettes like weapons.
> I am holding the side of the box where
> his hand is. My husband holds the other.
> Why is our boy in a box?
> A woman comes into the room. It is
> my mother. Why is her face so twisted?
> She has caught her daughter naked,
> in the act of making love.

The girls were wholly mystified. They were so literal, concrete, and I really loved this about them. I hadn't tried to do specific teaching about images or metaphors though; it was enough just to keep them writing and let them know how important writing had been and was in my own life. I hadn't wanted this to be a formal class, with the specifics of meter, stanza, line breaks—the mechanics of poetry writing—and they wouldn't have been interested in one, anyway. I just had to create the environment in which poems could evolve. The girls had a natural rhythm, were replete with profound material, and all had a troubled adolescent's yearning to be heard. I didn't have to preach or exhort them to higher ground, as my teachers had me.

I just had to show up. Over and over and over again. So they knew I was there for them. The rest just happened.

But now I found myself having go there in answer to Nia's questions.

"What does this mean, Sharon? Sex in a morgue?"

"No, well, yes, it's a metaphor—a comparison of two totally different things to make a point. The nakedness is my pain, the making love to a box—crazy idea but my son is in there—it's my attempt to say how big my love for him is, how desperately crazed I am to see him dead, how I don't believe it."

"Read more, Sharon!" said Tiffany. She'd understood, seemed dumbstruck.

"Stop staring at her, Tiffany," Brisa said."That's weird."

"I'm just looking at her watch," Tiffany shot back.

It always excited me when they really *got* something in one of the poems I read. But since the subject had been so abruptly changed, I just moved on, letting further explanations go.

"Let's write about death," I said. "You've all had an experience of that. It could be about the death of someone you love, or the death of a part of you, like a piece that died in a rape, or because of a violent boyfriend, or just about a relationship that ended. Or a death in your neighborhood, maybe. It really helped me, helps me, to write about Geoff's death, as a way of digesting it, taking it in, believing it is really true, letting my pain over it out."

"I'm in a good mood, I don't want it to go away," Nia said. "If I write about death I'll feel bad again."

I knew by now that ignoring their habitual protestations was usually more effective than trying to draw them out about them. And because of the trust we'd established, I felt okay about pushing them to take risks in their writing. More and more willing to do that, they all put pens to paper and pulled stuff up from wherever it had been stored in them.

When Nia began to read what she'd written about her stepfather dying, she broke into tears and couldn't finish. I took it from her and read the rest of it.

"Nia, this is powerful."

She got up and went to the bathroom, turned the water on to try to cover her prodigious sobs. Nadia wanted to go to her. "I want to be with her and help her, Sharon." Nadia looked at me for permission.

"Why don't you wait a bit, Nadia, then go and ask how, if, you can help. Sometimes people really need to cry. When we go to comfort them too fast, the feelings stop too soon. We need to really feel our feelings fully, so we can move through them and not get stuck."

They looked unconvinced. Hiram and Nadia, both nervous, moved toward the bathroom, but Nia came out before they got there.

Brisa wrote a poem that made me sure she'd thought of death a great deal. Mayra, who seemed to have forgotten about Bible class, wrote a moving piece about her Mami's death.

Grandma

she was my best friend
sisters through thick and thin
I miss her
she passed away through my hands
unmanageable

grandma
I couldn't handle when you left
I could talk to you about everything
I could cry on your shoulders
let my heart out to you

I used to do your hair
I loved your ocean blue eyes
I think you were loved greater than myself
my heart my soul

you had so much control over everything
you was the only thing that could calm me down
when I spent my baseball money only you knew
when I had my first boyfriend only you knew
when I had my first period
and I didn't know
and I was scared
you knew Mami

you helped me when I first shaved
when I shaved the wrong parts you laughed
but took care of her baby girl
who was itching like crazy

remember when I made you coffee
I didn't make it right
you was drinking the coffee
all that black stuff went in your mouth

abuela
you are the stars at night
the clouds that move through the sky
I feel your presence when I'm asleep

I Am Not a Juvenile Delinquent

> keep coming in my dreams
> thank you for helping me be me

I'd brought in more notebooks; there never seemed to be enough, mostly because the girls lost them so frequently. I didn't care. I had a carton of them I'd bought at Staples in the trunk of my car. They loved these notebooks for some reason, and it gave me great pleasure to have something I could give them that was so easy.

"Sharon, we want you to read from *Push* again, are you going to? Please!"

"Yes, of course, I was planning on it." I read a passage about Precious's bewilderment around the abusive relationship with her father.

> I feel so stupid sometimes. So ugly, worth nuffin'. I could just sit here wif my muver every day wif the shades drawed, watching TV, eat, watch TV, eat. Carl (her father) come over and fuck us'es.
>
> Go from room to room, slap me on my ass when he through...sometimes fuck feel good, that confuse me, everything get swimming for me...[2]

All the girls were protective of Precious, who was illiterate and unable to speak well, and was hugely overweight. She already had one baby by her father who had "down sinder" (Down syndrome), and was a virtual prisoner of her cruel and abusive mother, who was collecting welfare for Precious's child though the baby was being cared for by her grandmother. She was now pregnant for a second time, and being thrown out of school.

Nia wanted to borrow the book.

"I'll buy you a copy," I said.

"You don't have to do that, Sharon."

"I'd love to, Nia."

"Good work tonight, girls. Really good." I read *Push* until almost 9:00, when they had to leave for "hygiene" (showers and tooth brushing).

---

2   Pg. 35

"Ladies, you are so lucky to have this woman come here for you, even at night," Hiram said. "You should be thankful."

"I feel really lucky to be able to come, Hiram." And I did, tonight. The trip home crowded my mind as I drove. My thoughts were not of anxiety about the snow and ice, but about the girls, their poems and stories.

Tonight, for once, Geoff seemed far away.

Just Read, Sharon!

Despite my reluctance to teach writing poetry in a more formal way, Tiffany and Brisa had questions about writing poems, how to do it, exactly. Tiffany remembered everything I'd said, but wanted more instruction.

"Each word in a poem has to have emotional weight," I told her.

"What does that mean, Sharon?" she wanted to know.

"In a poem, you need to say things as economically as possible. I mean, in as few words as possible, let the reader know a lot with a little. It's a kind of condensation of experience. You know what I mean?"

"Not sure, Sharon."

"And a poem should surprise you, somehow. Leave you feeling different than you were before you read it."

"Okay, that I understand."

The other girls weren't as interested in learning more about what made a poem, I knew, and so I volunteered to meet with her another time and give her some books of poetry and talk more about all of this.

"Okay, Sharon, I would love that. When can we meet?"

"Let me talk to the staff and figure it out."

Tiffany was writing great stuff in our sessions. Here was one of her latest:

Prejudice

Our blood is the same—
so are our tongues.
We all breathe the same air
and like to have fun.
So what makes you different?
What makes you dislike me for the way I look,
the way I dress, the color of my skin,
or the way my momma cooks?

Why can't you see who I really am inside—
a person who loves, who hurts,
a person who gives, a person who cries.
All you seem to see is the color of my skin,
the size of my nose, the length of my hair.
When it comes to the weight of my heart
you really don't care.
Our outer layer doesn't really matter.
What's important is what's within.
Love your neighbor for what's inside.
Be their true friend.

The girls now pushed the furniture into a circle without being asked, and were sitting, expectant and ready, often eager to write.

Lesley reminded the girls that the "mission" in our group was self-expression, different from the mission of the larger community, which they recited on demand over and over again, much like the prayers my peers and I used to say in church and in class: *Promoting growth through responsible choices in our community.* Some of the girls, like Ana, had been conflicted about the differing standards in the larger community and in creative writing, especially the language dispensation.

The parlance in *Push* was pretty intense. I'd told them how necessary it was that Precious spoke in her own voice, the voice of an illiterate girl who had grown up hearing nothing but foul and abusive language, that she wouldn't sound like her true self otherwise.

"This is the gift of a writer, girls, to create a story, a picture, that relates a reality different from the one we know, or a deeper, broader one than what our own experience reflects. And the tool of language is what the writer uses to do that. How could Precious possibly have known how to speak and act normally, given her life?"

They weren't paying much attention to my attempt at instruction.

"Read *Push*, Sharon! We want to hear more about Precious. She's sixteen, why doesn't she just push him away? That's incest, eeuuw, her father." Nia and Mayra made faces.

"Maybe she can't." Nia was very protective of Precious. "She's scared, maybe she feels like she's at least getting some attention from somebody." I noticed Nia had the collection of Sapphire's poems I'd given her last week and was reading while we talked.

"I have a question for you. Why do you think the book is named *Push*?"

"Just *read*, Sharon."

"I will, but I want you to answer this question first, if you can."

"She's confused, Sharon," Tiffany said.

"Maybe because she pushed out the baby?" Mayra offered.

"Yes, that's great, what else?"

No one had any other ideas, so I offered some more.

"How about pushing out the writing? Pushing away the illiteracy? Finally, pushing away her mother?"

"Is Sapphire a lesbian, Sharon?" Nia wanted to know.

I should have known better, falling into the temptation of didactic mode. It was a guaranteed way for them to lose interest.

They were compelled by *Push*. I just gave in and read until the end of the session.

Show and Tell

It was late March now, and, maybe mistakenly, I thought the group was pretty settled in, coalesced. I'd been able to come each week after getting back from the retreat, and felt renewed and supported by the dharma talks I'd listened to and more sure of the fact that suffering was indeed an inescapable part of life and that accepting that was the letting go I needed so much. That feeling was short-lived.

At our next meeting I had what I thought was some pretty exciting news.

"Focus up, girls! I've been invited to give a speech about what it's like working here with you. There's a group called Connecticut Authors and Writers' Association that wants me to do this, on April 4. I tried to think of what I would say and suddenly it occurred to me that the answer was to bring you all with me and have you read your poems. A writer is supposed to 'show,' not 'tell,' so this makes sense to me. What do you think? Will you do it? They would be blown away by your wonderful work!"

"Sharon, I don't think I'll be able to come," Tiffany said. "I'm not on level."

Tiffany had stubbornly refused to move up from Level 2, which meant she couldn't go off-grounds or home on pass.

"There's plenty of time, Tiffany. You'll be able to get your level by then." I'd hoped this might be an encouragement for her. "And I'll have all your poems typed up, and we'll rehearse first. You must read your poem *Speak*, it's perfect for the beginning. You just have to come! We need this poem and need you to be the one who reads it."

Speak

Speak what you know
Speak it because you owe it to yourself
and to everyone else
Speak what you believe
Speak what you grieve

I Am Not a Juvenile Delinquent

Speak what you feel
Speak how you deal
Speak what you did
Speak it whether you're an adult or a kid
'cause words mean things
no matter who says what
So speak

"I'll take everyone out to dinner before. The meeting is at Tunxis Community College in Hartford."

I was getting more and more excited about it as I spoke, but there was not a corresponding enthusiasm in the girls. Mayra was sick and under her coat with her eyes closed for most of the session. Brisa looked out at me from the hood of her jacket, as usual. She was so beautiful, but dressed always in big, baggy, body-concealing clothes. There was so much hiding in that girl. How could I get the poetry out of her? I'd encouraged her to work on her poems, given her some suggestions. I now knew her brother was in prison for life, that he'd murdered two or three people and two dogs. One day I'd brought in *Doing Time*, a collection of prisoners' writings, and she'd wanted me to copy the whole book for her.

But Brisa never wrote about his incarceration, or wanted to talk about it. It was the other girls who had told me.

"How was your retreat, Sharon?" Tiffany wanted to know, moving closer to me, touching my arm. She was wearing a silky brown blouse with new jeans and black high-heeled boots, that gorgeous hair. I'd really wanted to give her some special attention, as we had discussed. She was just so talented and eager to learn. But when could that happen? There was never any extra time.

"Tiffany, thanks for asking. It was good, important for me to keep trying to take care of myself, try to let go of some of the grief. Writing helps so much, but these retreats do too."

Tiffany had a maturity and a presence that made her stand out from the other girls. Her anger still steamed, though, and I would soon find out what it was about from the poems she'd write.

"Read *Push*, Sharon, we want to hear what happens to Precious!" Nia pestered me.

"Listen, girls. I'll read some more and we will write, but for the next few sessions we have to practice for the meeting. You'll do it, won't you?"

"Okay, Sharon, but I bet they're not even going to let us go."

"Girls," Lesley said, "of course they will. You just have to stay on level, behave. And this is a privilege. Sharon is offering you something really special."

I was grateful to her for saying what I couldn't.

● ● ●

Now I was *really* anxious. Being a person who always jumped in fast, I had often volunteered for things without thinking of the consequences.

My volunteering had been a good thing, mostly, making me take risks that pushed me to grow, but getting from the concept to its actualization had always generated much stress. And these few weeks before the meeting would be no exception. I'd had no idea of all the pieces that would have to be in place to get the girls to the reading, never mind to actually give the reading. We'd need a staff that would make it all happen, an available van, enough girls on level, no crisis that day, getting everyone dressed, together, and out on time, finding the venue and the restaurant.

But at this point, I didn't know enough about what could go wrong to be as uneasy as I should have been.

At our next session, I waited at the top of the stairs in the house for the girls to come down. I was wearing a black knife-pleated skirt and Nia called me a "schoolgirl."

"Why are you wearing a skirt, Sharon?"

"All my pants are too tight, I need to lose some weight."

She patted my belly, gave it an appraising look, and agreed with me. Brisa said she had a stomachache and was too sick to come, but eventually showed up, wrapped in a big quilt. We trooped over to the dorm basement with Lesley.

What a difference it had made having her with us. She got the girls together, kept them enthused, and talked to them about the poetry group during the week, and about what a privilege it was for both her and them to have this program. A cheerleader. But she couldn't come to the reading at Tunxis; she'd be on vacation.

"I'll get Briana, to bring the girls, Sharon. She'll be good."

"Sharon, I know I won't be able to come," Tiffany said again.

"Tiffany, you have to open up, and show that you need others in your life," Nadia said. "Work in your treatment book."

"I don't want to get close to anyone here because I'm leaving soon. What's the point? I only talk to my family."

So this was the core of her resistance.

"Well, maybe it would make it easier to be here if you had some friends, Tiffany. But it's up to you. No one else can make these decisions for you. I understand why you don't want to be pressured. And selfishly, of course, I really want you to come. Anyway, let's get to *Push*."

I read the part about Precious leaving home and going to the shelter with her new baby and being robbed, and asked them to write about the worst thing that had ever happened to them. That was easy for me.

> *No! No! My husband is holding a telephone. I am standing at the kitchen counter watching him, wearing the long-sleeved tee shirt I'd slept in. It is the day before Mother's Day, 1987. No! No! He looks at me, puts the phone down, says Geoff is dead. No! No! You are lying, I say. I knew you would say that, he says, all color drained from his face. Here, you call. Here's the number. I grab the phone, dial the many numbers quickly. Hello Madame, the voice on the other end says. You told my husband a lie and I want the truth. I am sorry Madame, we have your son's ID, all his papers, his passport. No! No!*
>
> *The roof was falling on my head, the beams, the bricks, the nails were in my eyes. I couldn't see the tulips blooming outside the door. I couldn't see tomorrow, this afternoon, this morning. All the days hatcheted apart and thrown away. Oh my god. Oh my god. I am a mother and my son is dead. My mind is like a stone*

> *wall with no cracks. This fact cannot find its way in, no path*
> *opens, so I just watch it hanging in the air outside my mind.*

This was a hard prompt for them to do, maybe because they'd had so many "worse things" in their young lives. Tiffany wrote a fierce poem. *It was so good for her to be getting this anger out, I thought.*

My Heart Is like An Oven

My heart is like an oven
full of different kinds of foods
baking and burning—
now there's smoke coming from the stove.
My issues and problems are the food.
They're burning because they're hurting me.
The smoke is the pounding of my heart
full and ready to explode

I just don't want the oven to burn
the house down, but slowly the fire
is moving from room to room, destroying
gobs of furniture at a time.
How can I turn off the oven,
extinguish the fire?
I must, before the children burn
upstairs in their helpless sleep—
not knowing about the food
that was cooking.

All her writing came out as poetry. I never had to set it up differently when I typed it up.

Mayra thought Nia was being disrespectful when she read; they were all upset at Brisa's sleeping again. She was decidedly depressed, seemed to be returning to her shell, hiding under her hoodie and sweat pants. I continued to be worried about her. I'd brought in some collections of poetry for her and Tiffany to check out—*No More Masks, Cries of the Spirit*—but she didn't seem interested, just turned away and closed her eyes. Tiffany was, though, and took the books.

I'd brought pens for Nadia as she had asked me to, but she said they were too fat and hard to hold, so I gave them to Mayra and told Nadia I'd bring some thinner ones next week. Nadia wrote nothing today, saying she couldn't think of anything and was too depressed over two murders in her family since the last time we'd met. Her aunt and a cousin had been shot, both accidentally. Yet she couldn't think of the worst thing that had happened in her life!

Nia wrote but didn't want to read, and the others got mad. All of them were acting out today. I worried I'd been too permissive them in allowing that to happen so much. I continually tried to remember they were locked up here, and sometimes just needed to be teenagers and have some freedom to express themselves in speaking and behavior as well as writing in our group, freedom they did not in the daily program. But if I let that freedom go on too long, they got out of hand, sometimes taking advantage of me, and the session was lost to chaos. "Manipulating," they called it in Touchstone-speak.

Always I would struggle with this balancing act—the triple threat—firmness, boundaries, my resistance to being authoritarian—actually thinking I could find a formula that consistently worked. I could have saved myself a lot of anguish with a reminder of the certainty of impermanence, that things are constantly changing despite our efforts to control them.

But I was still far from a visceral acceptance of that fact.

Lesley was in and out of the room; there was a lot of pounding and noise coming from upstairs. One of the other residents had been violent and had to be in restraint mode, which meant being held down on the floor by three staff members until she was able to get control of herself and keep it.

As I drove back in the dark, all the events of the afternoon kaleidoscoped through my head, mixing liberally with the anxiety of preparing for the Tunxis reading. What had I been thinking, to take on this crazy project?

We Try Again

Only two more weeks to rehearse. The rest of the girls dribbled in with Lesley. Brisa stayed downstairs with Liz, her therapist, who brought her over later. Nia was always happy to see me, greeting me with a hug and some story about what had happened on her pass or at Touchstone that week, as she did today. Isabella gave me a soft smile, but Mayra was more low-key in her response, slower to hug and chatter.

I'd brought ten dollars' worth of pens in response to their request. They all fought over them, except for Tiffany, who stood aside, aloof.

I noticed, surprised, that most of the girls actually had brought their work with them, even in the plastic folders I'd distributed. Playing it safe, I'd brought copies, prepared for them to have left the poems in their rooms or at home after pass, as they so often did.

"Thank you for remembering your poems, girls. We're not going to write today, just rehearse."

"I have a court date in upstate New York, definitely can't come," Brisa reported.

This was puzzling. Upstate New York? It turned out that it was her brother's court date, the day he would get his final sentence, but I didn't know that then.

"She's lying, she just doesn't want to come," Mayra said.

"I'm scared," Brisa said. "I have low self-esteem. And I don't have anything to wear, anyway."

I had made some suggestions about clothing at our last meeting, saying maybe they could try something a bit more dressed-up than their daily attire, that was, if they had it. I knew many of the girls had to depend on the yearly $400 Department of Children and Families stipend for their needs. They didn't have families who could afford to buy them much, or were involved enough to go out with them and select clothing that fit, that they liked, and was flattering.

"Brisa, jeans are fine. I want you to be comfortable."

She seemed relieved.

Nia promised to dress up in a suit, and Mayra said she'd borrow something from her mother.

"Can my parents come?" Tiffany wanted to know, despite her protestations that she wouldn't be joining us.

"Of course, Tiffany. I'll get directions for them."

The girls confronted her, telling her she wasn't on level and had to work harder.

This was the kind of "positive peer pressure" that they emphasized here, getting the residents who were farther along in their treatment to influence the others to move up the level ladder. But Tiffany had continued to be resistant to all staff and resident beseeching to work on her levels, although she embraced the poetry group and the chance it offered to use her considerable talent.

Everyone was restless, nervous, talking and interrupting me and each other. Just getting a reading order was an ordeal. Finally one emerged. I wanted Tiffany to go first with her *Speak* poem. Even if she didn't come, maybe she'd allow someone else to read it. It would be perfect.

Mayra would go next, then Nia, Nadia, Isabella, and Brisa. They would then read *I Am Not A Juvenile Delinquent* as a group, taking turns.

"Why don't we read the last few lines together?" Nadia suggested.

"Marvelous idea!" I said. "But first, we have to go through the whole program."

It was impossible to hear them. Everyone mumbled and spoke too fast, looking down at the pages in their hands. I took one of Mayra's poems and recited it, demonstrating how to read more dramatically, project their voices, pause between the lines, look up at the audience, not drop their words at the end.

She got it right away and read much better next time. Nia was a natural performer; there were so many sexual references in her work, though, I wasn't sure how they'd be heard.

I had some idea of who would be in the audience—white, middle-class, all writers (I guessed from my attendance at one of the previous meetings)—

but I had little sense of how they'd react to the girls' explicit descriptions of their sexual experiences.

But I knew the work was strong, it had to be okay. It was going to be okay, I told myself. Nadia had such a beautiful voice, but her poem ended so sadly, *I don't like being me*. Tiffany was petulant, as usual, said she'd read, then that she wouldn't. Brisa read her poems but was dissatisfied with all of them. Isabella wasn't sure what to choose, then decided on a very moving poem about death, but her voice was so soft no one could hear her. They were querulous, rambunctious, and argumentative. Lesley and I were both incredibly frustrated with them.

"No one has to go, we'll just cancel it," I threw up my hands. "And I'm going home now, I'm tired of the way you all are behaving, I've had it."

"Oh, Sharon, don't leave. We'll try again." They read one more round, and this time it was perfect. Well, compared to last time, anyway. Ten minutes, just about right, I thought. And I'd have time to give a short introduction before their poems.

I spent the rest of our session reading *Push*; they wanted me to keep going until they found out if Precious had HIV. She did, and they were all as upset as if Precious were one of them.

Another Gorilla in the Mirror

At our next scheduled session, Lesley arrived just after I did, bouncing in enthusiastically, a pink baseball cap covering her honey-colored hair. She had such a positive attitude toward the girls and what I was trying to do with the poetry group. It was just so good to have her as an ally, to actually *have* an ally. Lori was supportive, but I never saw her; she was over the top with all the other stuff she had to do, managing the daily Touchstone crises and issues.

Much later, Lesley told me that Lori's supervisor hated me and the program and wanted to get rid of it, as did many others on the staff. In the weekly meetings where these adversarial discussions took place, Lesley had advocated constantly for it, insisting how was incredibly positive the poetry group was for the girls.

Nia was particularly edgy today. She was so volatile, and often seemed as though she was about to erupt. Because of her frequent outbursts, I surmised an assault charge might have brought her to Touchstone, though I was more inclined to staying unaware, wishing to meet each girl unlabeled.

I didn't know what charges had gotten the girls here, unless they had volunteered that information. And they mostly did, telling me of truancy, running away, drug use, selling drugs, prostitution, and assault, most always with justifications for their behavior, often ones which made a great deal of sense given their grim histories. Sometimes the girls were there because they'd been removed from their homes due to neglect, sexually or physically abusive parents, or because their mothers were in prison and they'd had nowhere else to go.

The judge decided their fates; in this era, though, most girls with charges were sent to seedy, shabby Long Lane, the official juvenile detention facility for the state of Connecticut (it later closed). Occasionally they were sent to York CI, the Connecticut women's prison, too harsh a place for young girls, though they'd be placed in a special unit. Touchstone's director and a staff clinician would go down and interview at Long Lane once a week, selecting those who might be good candidates for the more actively rehabilitative Touchstone program. Some of the girls told me all they'd done while incarcerated there was to sit on their beds and stare at the walls.

* * *

Mayra was calm, but complained of fatigue.

"I get a birth control shot every three months and it makes me so tired, Sharon. You know most of the girls here are on meds, and those pills make them really zonked out a lot of the time."

"There's no way I'm getting my level in time to come," Tiffany told me again.

"Are you sure, Tiffany? Lori told me that you could make it." I was angry and disappointed, having been so positive she'd get it together to join us and knowing how strong her poems would make the reading. But evidently there'd been some screw-up with her advocate. Each girl had an "advocate," someone who was supposed to be there for her when she needed help with program issues, or just someone to talk to, but everyone on staff was stretched so thin that what was supposed to happen in theory rarely did. And one advocate was assigned to several girls.

I told her I would call and try to straighten it all out.

Isabella read *It's Reality*. After last week's meeting, she'd slipped it to me, a torn-out notebook page, shyly asked me to look at it and tell her what I thought.

"Read it to me, Isabella," I'd said. Here's an excerpt:

> walking, walking late...scared walking lonely...footsteps...walk faster...two tall men...something over my mouth...clothes ripped off...beaten...I drift away... thought I was dead...so ashamed...face bruised...bleeding...open cuts...why me....it's rape...

"We have to make sure the world hears this poem," I'd said, tears running down my face. The other girls had been quiet, awed by its raw power. I was discovering that they knew little about each other and what they wrote in our group was revelatory. Even their therapists didn't know much of what they shared here.

Brisa wasn't here. She actually had gone to her brother's sentencing. They'd been afraid she wasn't going to come back; she did, finally, but high. Lori had told me she'd been subjected to a great deal of physical and sexual abuse. The girls told me she was struggling. I knew she was. Sometimes I thought there was no escaping their trauma; the crippling that ensued for them was like losing a limb, sometimes two.

"How do you feel, girls, if I describe Touchstone at this meeting as a place for girls who are on probation?"

All of them but Nia were okay with that. She was proud. She did not want her incarceration known, and would not relent.

"No one is listening to me," she said.

"We are listening, Nia, but you are in the minority."

I wasn't sure how hard she'd stick to this position, so I decided to just let it go for the time being. We rehearsed again and they were so much better than they'd been before, except for one big thing—they laughed and smiled inappropriately while reading intensely painful pieces.

"Girls, that spoils the power of your delivery, try not to do that." I knew they were nervous, but hoped they wouldn't laugh at the reading. I didn't want to make a huge deal about it now.

"You're going to take us out to dinner before, right, Sharon?"

"Yes, I told you I would. We'll have a nice dinner, I promise."

This whole project was assuming such gigantic size in my life that I was having major surges of anxiety all the time and had no room in my mind for anything else. I hadn't any idea how it would go, and imagined all kinds of calamities. As it turned out, I would be right in my imaginings, not only in this first effort, but in many others.

If I'd ever wanted a practice ground for my intention to see Pema Chodron's "gorilla in the mirror" more clearly, I couldn't have picked a better one than Touchstone.

Cathedral

For forty-five full, long, minutes, I waited, sweating, almost hyperventilating, at Rossini's, the restaurant where we'd agreed to meet for the big night. No girls. I *knew* I'd given the right directions.

I ordered a vegetable pizza, reasoning that I had all their work with me and if the worst happened and they didn't show, I could just read the poems myself. As my pizza arrived, so did they.

"The staff meeting ran late," Briana, the staff member assigned to the girls that night, told me, without apology. I knew if it had been Lesley she would have left anyway to be on time, no matter what objections anyone had raised. But Lesley was on vacation.

"We'll have to rush," I said, half furious, half euphoric that they had really shown up. "Two large pizzas, half cheese, half pepperoni," I called to the waitress. "We're in a hurry."

"We want buffalo wings, Sharon!"

"Okay, buffalo wings, and sodas all around. Girls, I am so glad you're here!"

Mayra sat down first. She was wearing an obviously new black leather jacket over a very low cut tank top, khaki pedal pushers, and big white mules. Nia pushed in next to me. She had on a skin-tight bright magenta suit and classy black pumps.

Nadia wore a hat, a stretchy tube top that barely covered her breasts under a white shirt, and a long blue skirt with the same white mules Mayra wore. She looked like she was going to the beach. Isabella had made it, but Tiffany had not, as predicted.

"Girls, you all look absolutely beautiful!"

When the pizza and wings arrived, everyone piled their plates and ate fast.

We took the leftover pizza with us in a box, arriving at Fisher Hall exactly at 7:00. Out of breath from rushing, the girls, Briana, and I walked into a typical college conference room filled with plastic molded chairs in rows, enough for a good-sized crowd.

Only a few were filled.

"Where is everyone?" I said, thinking maybe I'd gotten the time wrong. "Where is the audience?"

I didn't have the time wrong. There were eleven people, counting Briana, the other presenter and me. I was livid. Where was the audience for my girls?

I couldn't bear to see them hurt and let down, as I was sure they would be.

The other presenter gave her brief talk about using writing sessions to work with victims of domestic violence, and then I was on. The girls sat next to me at a table in the front of the room.

> Working as a writing teacher/coach/mentor with the girls of Touchstone has been one of the most exciting experiences of my life. I was asked here tonight to tell you about it, but nothing could let you know better than to listen to the girls themselves. So here are Nia, Mayra, Nadia, and Isabella, to share their wonderful poems with you.

I looked out. At least everyone was paying attention.

The girls stood and read with magnificent presence, as though the room was packed with people dying to hear their every word. The small audience was galvanized. My anger melted away. It was as if I'd lost myself totally and was inside of them, somehow, feeling and watching and glowing from within their skin.

After they finished, the audience crowded around them. The secretary gave them mugs embossed with "CT Writer-Authors Guild," and the girls acted like they'd been given trophies. Another member asked them to be on his cable TV show. A teacher wanted them to come and read to her class. Isabella was crying. Everyone was getting and giving hugs. That conference room had become a cathedral, infused with beauty and truth, peopled by rapturous pilgrims bound together in open-hearted humanity.

The other presenter came back with us to Rossini's and we all celebrated with big bowls of ice cream, even getting the grouchy-faced waiters to smile and heat up our leftover pizza, which tasted just perfect with the mint chocolate chip. I drove home in a dream, deciding by the time I'd arrived at my red farmhouse that we must do another public reading. I would heavily publicize it so we'd have a much bigger audience.

I now absolutely knew their voices *had* to be out in the larger world.

The next day I called a friend who was on the board of Artwell, a small art gallery in Torrington, not far from Litchfield, and asked her if she would ask the director if we could have a reading there in June. The word came back quickly: "Sure."

I began planning for it right away.

"My File"

When I came the next week, I tried to get them to talk about our triumph of the week before. They seemed to have forgotten all about it and how they'd felt afterwards. The glow of accomplishment was completely gone.

I would come to know this recurring aftermath much more acutely in the years ahead, when I would arrive at Touchstone a week after a grand off-campus success and find the girls spinning into some current catastrophe, absorbed with its thorns, which were so much more compelling to them than any past experience. They mostly lived totally in the present, though their devastating pasts often unconsciously informed that present.

From my therapy training, I knew that traumatized people often sought to repeat the experience of trauma over and over, as a kind of masochistic comfort. Their crises and clashes with each other, staff, and families surely did that. But I also knew that telling one's trauma story was a necessary part of healing, so despite the chaos of the moment, I persisted in pushing for more exposure.

"Well, girls, I've made a big decision. I hope you'll agree with it. Tell me what you think. You were so great at Tunxis that I think we have to do more readings."

I said I'd talked to some people in Torrington at the Artwell Gallery and they'd love us to give a reading in June. And that we'd been invited by Suzanne Heyd to be guests at her poetry classes at Danbury High in a few weeks.

"Are there boys there?" Nia wanted to know.

"Yes, Nia."

"And the guy who wanted you on his TV show is waiting to get permission from your parents and parole officers."

"Oh, all our parents will say yes!" They looked really excited about that. TV was such a major and familiar aspect of their culture that they were able to understand what would be required of them in a way they did not for the readings.

Lori also had to get permission from Long Lane, I wasn't sure why. But I knew she'd do it.

Isabella looked blank and flat, probably from all the medication she was on. Lesley had told me she'd been hospitalized for a suicide attempt during the week.

"Why is she back so soon?" I had wanted to know.

"Oh, they just stay there for a few days, get their meds adjusted."

"That's all? No group therapy, no family therapy?"

"Nope. They send them back here as soon as they can."

"Come on, Sharon, stop talking. We want to write!" Nadia reminded me of our primary purpose. Once I'd begun the outside readings, I had trouble keeping the balance between the time-consuming event planning and writing sessions. I knew the readings were valuable to the girls, but I didn't want to shortchange our writing periods with all the preparation.

Balancing the competing issues would be a continuing dilemma for me, one that I was never able to resolve.

"You're right, Nadia. Thanks for giving me that kick in the behind. Let's get started." I read a section of *Push* in which her social worker left the room and Precious took the file from her desk and read it.

> Soon as she close the door behind her I'm up. Moving fast, quiet...nervous, I can smell my sweat stinking...yup, here it is, Jones, Clareece P...I fly back to big green chair, stuff file in my backpack.[3]

"Write about your file. What's in it." I didn't know how I would ever top this book for material that engaged them so.

"Oh, that's a good one, Sharon," Nia said.

Brisa lay on the floor to write and all the girls challenged her, told her that was the same as sleeping. Mayra didn't have her notebook, so I gave her paper. Isabella suddenly snapped awake and began to write.

---

3   Pg. 116

I Am Not a Juvenile Delinquent

I struggled to think of how I'd write about mine. "Keep your pen moving," I always told the girls. "Just write the first thing that comes into your head."

> Street life, drugs? I never had any but my husband's brothers did, running away as teenagers to our house in the Hudson Valley in the '70s, planting a marijuana garden in back of the barn where I would never see it, hiding the crop in plastic bags in the freezer behind the venison our neighbor gave us and that we would never eat.
>
> No one much in my college days did drugs. We all drank scotch and smoked cigarettes. There were plenty of times I drank too much and got sick.
>
> I guess, more than any drug, I have struggled with control—trying to think I can fix everything—I have felt that things would only be all right if I worked hard to make them so. My son's death put how wrong I was in my face. My brothers-in-law taught me so much by sharing their growing up and drug experiences with me. Mark got hepatitis C in Mexico and came to us, yellow and sick, to recover. They all worshipped Guru Maharaj-ji, meditating in their ashram with sheets over their heads, which my kids found fascinating and totally weird. Pot was their daily drug of choice, and I often found the ends of the hand-rolled joints in the ashtrays in our house back then.
>
> I wished their lives could have been different, but their lives were their lives and all I could do was to be there for them, love them, listen to them, and not judge. Those were crazy times (the '70s)— people did crazy things; everyone, it seemed, was trying drugs, sleeping with their best friend's wife or girlfriend, leaving their marriages, wearing suede hot pants (I had a green pair)—trouble is, we don't always know we're being crazy when we are. That takes mistakes, falling on our faces, other people telling us we're screwing up but standing by to hold our hands as we recover.

● ● ●

It was April already. "I have attention deficit disorder and I need you all to focus up!" Mayra told us, chomping on a chocolate rabbit at our next meeting. One of the clinicians wanted to sit in with us, but Mayra wouldn't let her—said she didn't feel comfortable with her there. I'd brought in jellybeans and they all ate from their Touchstone Easter baskets as we talked and wrote.

Isabella was sitting next to me; she seemed so pleased with how I'd reconfigured her poem into stanzas, but Nia was jealous.

"I think you like Isabella's writing better than mine!" she asserted loudly.

I was stunned. "Why, Nia?"

"Because you wrote her a letter."

"But I did it because she gave me her poem to type, and I wanted to tell her how I had edited and shaped it. Girls, what do you think? Do you agree that the note I wrote on her poem makes it seem like I like Isabella's writing better than Nia's?"

There was a loud chorus of no's. Nia seemed satisfied.

"Okay, moving on. Danbury High tomorrow." I was nervous about the language in their stories and their length—they all wanted to read the ones they'd written last week, on their files. I didn't want to discourage them, but Nadia's was full of "bitch, shit, fuck," Nia's was a poignant telling of a girl who has a life in the street but wants to connect with her mother.

"Let's all reread what we wrote last week and see how it sounds, okay?" It went slowly. They all wanted me to read mine again too, the recounting of my brothers in-laws' drug exploits in the '70s.

"I know what you mean, Sharon," Tiffany said, "about wanting to control and fix everything. I'm the same way." We talked some about how hard it was to give this problematic habit up. She seemed relieved that we had the same issue. This was one of the things I loved about being with the girls in this way, not as a therapist. I could share experiences from my life that matched theirs. I could give them my humanity.

"I don't know how I can continue to be an independent, free-thinking person and not a robot mouthing Touchstone 'mission' jargon when I go home," she said.

I concurred with her that this was a valid concern.

"I don't agree with you at all, Tiffany." Brisa was in a rare talkative mood today. "We need the mission to help us when we get out."

"Everyone is entitled to have their own opinions, girls. We have too much to do to get ready for tomorrow to get into this. Let's talk about it another time. Tiffany's going for her level so she can come to Danbury with us. Let's support her."

Driving home, I wondered if I was getting too attached to these girls. A life without them seemed unimaginable.

Mixing It Up

It was a long trip to Danbury High in the van, and hot for April. Mayra was in a terrible mood; she'd already had a time-out that morning, and there had even been a question about her being able to come, fortunately resolved in our favor. Lesley had advocated hard for her and our group; this was another great advantage to having a consistent assistant on campus. She knew the importance of our field trips for the girls.

All of them had dressed up, though the long skirts on three of them were quite tight. Nadia wore a fuchsia shirt, just stunning with her skin tone. Nia had donned glasses, a leather jacket over a striped top, and capris.

Isabella was nervous. I tried hard to comfort her with reassurance and a hug.

"Mayra will read for you if you feel you just can't, sweetie." I told her, my hand on her shoulder. I was amazed and proud and of course, anxious as usual, that they planned to read such revealing work to kids their age, and hoped the Danbury students could handle it appropriately.

Suzanne had arranged for some girls from her advanced class to meet my group at the door and have lunch with us in a small room off the cafeteria. White and middle-class to the hilt except for T-Shaun, a tiny black girl with cornrows, they greeted us enthusiastically and gathered about the lunch table, chattering about poetry, college, and classwork with an easy assurance. They seemed genuinely interested in drawing out the Touchstone girls, who silently ate their burgers and fries.

I wanted to wrap them in a big protective cloak so they wouldn't get hurt, however inadvertently, by these confident, untroubled girls.

"What do you read?" asked one of them brightly, looking at Mayra.

"We don't like to read," she said.

"We don't read poetry," Nia added with a challenging stare.

"Is it getting to be time for class?" I asked, worried that more difficult questions would be coming. "Must be."

The class was mostly female, mostly white, the crème de la crème of the largest public high school in Connecticut. I introduced the Touchstone girls, explaining how the use of their own language was integral to their writing. I said that they did not speak in "dead white male" as many of the poets the class studied did.

The students seemed stunned as the girls read. I was tense, sweating, on the edge of my chair, not sure at all how this would go over, though I knew Suzanne well and was pretty sure she could handle any fallout.

It's going on too long, I worried. *Their stories are taking up too much time.*

Mayra read this:

Weed Ganja, Chocolate Buddha, Alize Bacardi, Wet Caskin Cream

Weed was my girl,
Mary Jane was my girl.
When I was bored
she was there. She
brought excitement
to my life. She brought
adventure. The others
were my main thing.
They made me feel all right,
They made my heart sing.
Alize just tasted good.
Bacardi just blow me away
Straight vodka made me
want to have fun. I keep
going and going

"You all know what Mary Jane is, don't you?" Mayra asked.

The kids laughed nervously in affirmation. "You are amazing to write anything like that! I could never do it," one girl responded. "All of this could be a book." They were astonished that such personal stories could be read. Suzanne asked them to write their reactions for homework and said she would send them to us.

The next class had kids more like my girls in it. Two girls in the front row wearing tight jeans and low-cut tops listened raptly, as did a dark-skinned boy in a leather jacket. Sensing the intense attention, Nia and Mayra read extra pieces. Isabella shyly told everyone she was scared before she read; I touched her arm several times as she recited It's Reality in a shaky voice, and she smiled at me.

This was a class that had been discussing alternatives to violence; Suzanne asked if my girls thought writing might be one.

"There is so much stuff running around in my head at night," Nia told them. "Writing it down really helps me."

Isabella said the same thing, and Mayra talked about writing as an alternative to smoking or hitting, though defended assault when it was in self-defense.

"Think of the consequences," Nia added. "You wouldn't want to have to say you were a felon on a job application." I never knew what was going to come out of her mouth, but she almost always nailed it.

A volatile stew of emotions jolted me. I was proud and sad at the same time, proud of today's profound achievement, but sad all over again at what they'd suffered. I'd never seen the girls read or interact in front of kids their own age who lived in a world altogether outside their sphere.

On our way out, boys thronged them. One hit on Isabella immediately after her emergence from the ladies' room, another one pressed snapshots of himself on Mayra. I saw her writing down her name and address for him and said nothing, wondering what was drawing the boys to my girls—their difference, this new vibe, I supposed, was a great allure, I thought with some cynicism and protectiveness. Of course, they were beautiful, and had written and read openly about their sexual experiences, which possibly contributed to the attraction. I hoped that was not the case, though it was hard not to imagine it could be.

I was glad we were getting out of there. I didn't feel they were as safe with boys as they'd been with the girls.

In the van going home, Lesley and I talked of social work, her father, her life and future plans. The girls alternated between sleeping and singing to the radio. I told them that they all had music burning inside them and their poems brought it out.

I had lost myself in their beautiful, soothing voices.

Part II

My Girls

*"Love takes off masks we fear we cannot live without
and know we cannot live within."*

—James Baldwin

Raindrop in a Gale

I think it was around late spring that first year that I began referring to the girls as "my girls." Of course, I knew "girls" could be considered a politically incorrect term, as they were really properly young women, but "girls" seemed right, somehow, mixing my love for them with our large age difference. And it wasn't that I felt possessive of them or responsible for them; in fact, it was a relief that they were here in the sheltered structure of Touchstone and I could leave and not worry about their emotional or physical safety. It was more that I felt profoundly linked to them through the sharing of our stories. The "me and them" had become an "us" as we all took off our masks with pen and paper, voice and vulnerability.

My life had fallen into theirs.

Katherine Boughton, a local newspaper reporter, had written a profile of me for the *Litchfield County Times*, in a weekly section on people doing interesting things in our region. It was titled, appropriately, I thought, *Raindrop In A Gale*, a direct quote from me describing how I felt working at Touchstone. The interview had demanded reflection. It seemed clear that surrendering the hope or idea that I could really change anything was essential knowledge I needed to absorb.

The Ugly American, by Eugene Burdick and William Lederer, was a book I'd read in the late '50s about the arrogance of Americans going into foreign countries with the certainty of missionaries bearing the values that would "save the cannibals" (a memorable if coarse phrase I'd heard used by one of my first family therapy teachers, Carl Whitaker, admonishing us to avoid that distorted concept when treating clients). It told of the need to first listen to and interact with the people of those cultures and countries, to discover what could be actually beneficial to them, before offering assistance or ideas they couldn't utilize.

The lessons of that book had come with me into my adult life, as an educator, family therapist, and writing teacher. They had been challenging to implement, as hope of effecting change in the unjust world had driven me for years. But my grief over Geoff had worn me down, forced me to find a different vision, to struggle with my limitations, the humility I didn't have. The girls had become my teachers, with their life stories, their constant resistance to my careful plans, their weekly invitation to surrender to what was.

I needed to give up the attempt to control that had been so central in my life.

At some level, I guess I had always known I was just that raindrop in a gale. In the hurricane-force winds of their lives, I was the tiniest of specks. This awareness helped me to persevere, as did the tenacity that was part of my habit and personality structure. Some intuitive instinct told me I just had to keep showing up; that's what mattered most to my girls.

By persisting this long, I'd outlasted everyone's certainty that I would be a fly-by-night. And I intended to continue. I was sure I was getting more out of being at Touchstone than it was getting from me.

"My Story"

Someone had sent me an article on the Women In Prison Options Program from a publication called *Doubletake*, and in it was a compelling piece by an inmate, called simply *My Story*. At our next session, I read it to the group and asked that they do as the author had.

"Tell everything, like she did, girls, drugs and all. Title it *My Story*, like she did." I knew they'd committed many of the same offenses this inmate had, and experienced much of the same trauma.

Brisa said she was not coming, then that she would. Isabella wanted to leave.

"Lesley, please tell Brisa, if she comes, she must commit to coming every time," I implored, frustrated once again with all their indecision and chaos.

Finally they settled down, warmed to the task, and were still writing after a half-hour. This time their stories tapped the deepest wells of horror in their lives, with such raw power. Nadia, dark hair falling into her face, began to cry as she read of being gang-raped and having her body savagely violated. Nia went to sit next to Isabella as she began to tell of monstrous abuse, rape, and drugs. Mayra wrote of Mary Jane, blunts, drive-by shootings, rapes, and slashed tires, Nia of her street life and how badly she wanted her mother's acceptance. Brisa wrote nothing but listened intently. Tiffany told of seeing her mother beaten over and over again, of her own constantly flaming anger.

Melanie, a new girl, wrote of how her mother had abandoned her to a grandmother, a frequent occurrence for the Touchstone girls. She was fourteen and had been "in the system" for years.

> When I was eight, I started to get raped. I had so much hate towards the guy that did the rape. I used to hate going to Grandma Rose's house because he was around. Yes, he was the guy who had raped me, yes, I call him #1. I felt upset because he took something I had cherished, that I'd been saving for a long time—only eight years wasn't enough.

At the age of ten I was the so-called "slut"—"look who's around" they'd say—Green-Eyes's little sister—I was bad—always wanting to get with all the teenagers who weren't even mature. I was growing too fast, I was only ten. Questions about sex, love, men, girls, drugs, cops—you ask me, I knew the answer. I got immune to getting raped all day, all the time. I used to hate it.

At the age of eleven I had my so-called fiancé. He basically gave me the world. I was young but I knew how to get down, give boys what they wanted from this girl. I was mature and looked older, but eventually I told the boys my age and they were like—"for real—damn—that young-ass girl!" Me and my fiancé Miguel were in love—yeah, probably you think at the age of twelve I don't know about love—yeah, you right—but I had my own perspective about love—you caring about me, always, no matter what happens, being there for me, always buying me the things I need, showing me the love that I felt I needed.

By the age of twelve and a half I had on my neck nothing but pearls and jewelry—of course my mom didn't care about me. She was an addict of pot, weed, whatever you wanna call it. She will never answer the phone—hardly come to see me—too busy getting ready for her next mate—which she was getting paid for. I don't know how it feels even now to say this. Can I introduce you to "my mother"—no. My "wanna be" mother—that's what I would usually call her—a bitch—I have so much hate because I really needed her when I was going through some shit with my grandmother. This fucking lady didn't let me do anything. I was always cooking, cleaning, washing, buying, selling, and baby-sitting. I never had the opportunity to go outside and be with my friends for a couple of hours—because this lady will be so bitchy. She used to always yell at me—talking about "don't let me catch you with her or him because you know what they bring."

"Please Grandma, don't fucking assume," I used to tell her. I can't believe we are even related.

I always used to say I got dumped in the trashcan and picked out of it by a crack head. My life's been miserable—there's no other way I can say it because it just is. Now I'm only fourteen with a whole lot ahead for me. I'm just hoping someday I'll be a mother and I'll be able to give my child what was never given to me—

I Am Not a Juvenile Delinquent

which is a lot—just remember this is not all the whole story.

Hers was a narrative I was to hear repeatedly in the years I worked at Touchstone. These tales never failed to clench my heart and often, to make me cry in our sessions. There was a fine line to walk, though, between human compassion and overdoing an empathetic response; the latter could make the girls feel self-conscious about their issues and turn our group into a kind of therapy session or discussion of problems better saved for another more private time.

I tried to stay aware of the potential for these accidental sorties. Though my therapy training and experience was certainly useful, I was ever cognizant of the fact that our gatherings had been defined as a writing group rather than a clinical one, a safe place for taking risks in speaking the truths of our lives without feedback or judgment. But sometimes compassion and tears were the only authentic response.

Even Lesley had written a powerful piece today. These were the best of the year. I was a little scared for them at the tender and perilous areas everyone had so willingly explored—but then, I reasoned, look at the dangerous risks they had already taken in their lives. This risk had a different kind of potential—one for healing, even transformation.

"Girls, girls, I am so sorry that your lives have given you such suffering. You are so brave to share these stories with me and each other. Please be kind to yourselves now as you go back to the larger community, give yourselves some space and tenderness. Lesley, can you take extra special care of them tonight?"

"Yes, Sharon, I will."

They were quiet as they lined up to leave.

Black Queens

Arriving for our meeting in early May, I got buzzed in, and right away saw Isabella in the hall.

"I can't come, Sharon, I have a doctor's appointment," she told me, looking down at the floor.

Lesley gathered the girls and we were able to go back to the dorm basement. Nadia looked terrible, flat, like she was in pain but didn't know it. Mayra seemed soporific again, and Nia complained she was getting a migraine. Tiffany was wheezing and needed an inhaler. Hiram finally brought it. Brisa sat silently on the couch. I caught myself thinking that maybe she'd surprise me and write something this week.

Dream on, Sharon.

Suzanne had asked her Danbury High students to write responses to hearing the girls read a few weeks ago. I began reading them aloud.

> *I really had no idea of what the real world was like. Of course, I've sat through countless drug ed and health classes, watched tons of movies and listened to boring lectures on the consequences of using drugs, but nothing has ever touched me as much as your poems did. These poems should all be in award-winning books receiving praise from critics all over the country. They are heart-felt, non-censored accounts of experiences you have been through, things that I couldn't have imagined...I realized that I am not really a part of the real world but rather of my own small little world, hidden from all the dangers outside (of it).*

The girls were awed, impressed, then tried to guess who had written what.

"That's from Erica, that bubbly happy girl. Remember, Lesley? She reminds us of you."

Lesley was chagrined at first to be characterized that way, but then said she realized they had a point. The girls got so much programmatic conversation and rejoinder from the staff, so little that was real, that I could see that it must be refreshing for them to have Lesley with us in this different, much more relaxed and human capacity. She obviously enjoyed it too, and supported us wholeheartedly until she left Touchstone for another job.

"Here are some more, girls."

> *Gone are the days when I could set you aside and say conveniently 'not my problem' as you suffer, succeed, live... gone are my preconceived notions about life...gone is my apathy towards the world.*

> *The admiration in the room for these "black queens" went through the roof. Their graceful dignity and surviving ambition to be better than what they had faced is like a candle in a dark room that got brighter with each girl's voice and words...such a wonderful experience.*

> *You guys were different from all the guest speakers that we've had this year, there was just something more that was there that really created a fresh vibe in here.*

I asked them for a reaction. What did they think, feel?

"We're tired, Sharon," Nadia and Mayra said in unison.

"Come on, you must feel something."

They acknowledged being surprised, shocked even, at what the kids had written. They hadn't imagined having had such an impact. I had to keep remembering the abysmal self-esteem that lurked under their defiant exteriors.

"See how your words move people?" I said. "That's why our reading at the art gallery in Torrington is going to be so great. Writing is a way to connect with others—to feel powerful in a different way than you can from looking good, catching men."

"Well, I'm glad we helped people," Nia said.

"I've got some poems written by women prisoners today, girls. I'll read them and then we'll use some as prompts. I think you'll relate." Some, written by a woman named Q-Nora, were really, really angry. The girls were taken by these and quickly began to write about "a time I was angry."

Nadia wrote about why she was not angry.

"I've never been angry," said Brisa, looking me square in the eye. At my other suggestions of feeling possibilities, she denied feeling anything at all.

"Why don't you write about why you're not angry, like Nadia?" Tiffany suggested.

"Nope."

Clearly Brisa was not going to write today or any other day. I couldn't imagine why she kept coming, unless someone, maybe her advocate, was insisting she did. Any other reason was thoroughly veiled to me.

But anger was an emotion I'd struggled with all my life. I remembered my father shaking his finger in my adolescent face one day, saying in an enraged voice, "You're so angry!"

"Of course I am angry, Daddy," I'd wanted to say though the words were inchoate then. "I'm angry with the criticisms you constantly heap on me, the don'ts and the no's to what I want and need. I'm angry with you, how you never come home, how you're so cruel to our mother, how you yell at me when I am reading and tell me to go and sweep the terrace. I'm angry because I have no freedom to wear what I want, do what I want, say what I need to say. I'm angry because you are always telling me what I shouldn't be, never supporting what I am."

As an adult, I had been quick to anger, quick to express it, unlike so many other women, definitely the women with whom I'd worked in therapy, to whom anger was so frightening.

"Anger is energy," I'd say to them." It can move you forward, help you change your life. And under that anger is often hurt, we need to look at that too." There were so many reasons for female rage, so many reasons to repress it.

So my pen, too, flew across the page.

After the planes, the taxis, the morgue, we walked up Via Veneto

I Am Not a Juvenile Delinquent

past the Franciscan Monastery where the bones of all the dead monks were arranged in bouquets, hearts and other weird designs, glued to the walls like decorations. Some surrounded a sign that said "as you were I once was, as I am so you will be"— we'd been there with him, I remembered it. The embassy was next door. They frisked us going in. They x-rayed our bags. My mother was perspiring in her linen suit and white sneakers. The curl was coming out of her hair. My husband held out his keys, Swiss army knife, defeated, tired. Matthew—I don't remember what he did. They opened my camera and looked inside it. I don't think I said anything but I was screaming inside. Goddammit, our son is dead. We're only here because you made us come. Just let us in and get this over with. I'd rather be home in my house in Connecticut right now waiting for him to fly back from this cursed country that claimed him, claimed his life, then here in this place.

No, no, no, I wanted to yell at the guard, but I didn't. I had to be the polite US citizen to get what I wanted, my son's body flown back to the states. We trooped upstairs. The wood was dark, shiny. The building was old, elegant, marble. Someone showed us to the embassy official's office, the one that talks to US citizens whose children have died, I guessed. A stuffy, officious man in a dark suit, he wanted to get rid of us as fast as possible, but pretended to offer help. The police were investigating Geoff's death. An American citizen abroad, a bad thing politically.

Asthma, he said, it was probably his asthma medication mixed with alcohol, he had been drinking. He acted like Geoff had been drunk and that's why he died, I wanted to take his tie and wrap it right around his neck, pull it as tight as I could until his eyes popped out of their sockets and flew across the room. Geoff had had a half-bottle of wine, that's all. Matthew looked at me, making sure I saw his next move. He took the gum he was chewing out of his mouth and stuck it under the thick brown office chair he sat on.

I'd spent the whole day before I'd come down today getting posters made and cards addressed for the Artwell performance in two weeks, making calls to anyone I could think of to get them to come. At some point I remembered the anniversary of Geoff's death was this weekend, Mother's Day.

The memories of it were in my bones and blood, oozing out in a commemorative hemorrhage as spring returned and May 9 approached.

I went to hug Brisa before I left. She turned away from me.

Attached to Outcomes

The next week Brisa dropped out. I guess she just couldn't take the constant exposure to feelings this group had become all about. She was an impenetrable girl, perhaps even more complex and traumatized than the others. I'd never been able to reach her, and felt like a total failure because of that, despite all my high-minded attempts to grasp the fact that I was impotent, and most of what happened in our group was accidental, that I was that "raindrop in a gale," an insignificant speck in the high winds of Touchstone.

Here was hard evidence of that and I hated it.

Tiffany had been on time-outs all day and was really struggling, but she came. I read more from *Push*, a scene with the counselor about Precious's earliest memory, and a long section about the mother's explanation about why the abuse happened—with very graphic sexual images—but there was not much time for writing with all the stuff I had to go through about our upcoming TV, radio, and Artwell performances.

The girls were excited this time, but I wasn't. My gut was a mess, I was losing my temper with John over nothing, I had a dream of mislaying my wallet on my way to a poetry reading that I was late to give; when I got to the venue, I found I'd forgotten my poems. I worried about everything—audience size, behaviors, cooperation from Touchstone, how they'd be received.

The next week we gathered at the UConn radio station on the Torrington campus, where a friend had a weekly show. I hadn't been sure coming was the greatest idea, but my friend really wanted to support us and thought it would be great publicity for Artwell. The six of us crammed into the tiny studio. The girls passed mikes back and forth, stretching over each other. They missed words, dropped papers. If "fuck" was in the poem, they were supposed to take it out and substitute another word. They all forgot to do this. Isabella was fantastic. Nia's writing was strong, but she read hesitantly. Mayra blew us all away with this one:

A Woman Speaks to Ignorance

There ain't nothing wrong with me giving my opinion.
There ain't nothing wrong with crying over your dumb ass.
I ain't got nothing and you, you got it all, so why is you
trying so hard stuffin' silence down my mouth
like it's the third course to the best meal I ever tasted?
And if that's the meal, what's my dessert?
I done suffered in silence too long for you
to tell me the speech I speak is wrong.
I'm older and I'm wiser, I done seen all the tricks,
I know the minds of the world and
what they think.
First you were under my skin tone and abused me.
God knows the things I've been through. I've been beat,
raped and left to die, and you go free. I pray it ain't me
that you'll get again but now things done been turned
around
and I will no longer hang my head to the ground with shame.
I will walk one day with pride. I will walk with proud strides.
I will keep on, I will not quit, I will not die, I will keep on
living.
I will try no matter what. I am a woman, I cannot die.

I knew this poem would have to be part of the Artwell reading.

Tiffany had been disrespectful to a teacher and was denied the privilege of being with us, and her parents hadn't yet given permission for her to be at the TV station with us next week. But she'd shared a stunning poem revealing abuse by an uncle, a real breakthrough for her.

We had all encouraged her to read it with the audience as her witness, at Artwell.

Beauty the Enemy

I'm ashamed because you used me.
I'm hurt because you abused me.

I'm sad because you're glad.
You're glad because of the fun you had.
You made me feel worthless.
You used me for sexual services.
You've killed my self-respect.
It all happened because of neglect.
When my heart was just healing,
You never gave a damn about my feelings.
You made everything worse.
Your existence is a curse.
My heart and body feel so torn.
My head aches. My heart is sore.

All my eyes can do is cry.
All my head can do is wonder why.
Your words and actions run through my brain.
Please help me...I'm going insane.
Why did you do this to me?
You made beautiful a bad thing to be.

There was just not enough time to rehearse. The TV show, finally scheduled, would be a help. A friend volunteered to come down early the night of the performance and set up the mike, help the girls practice with it. Each day my mind struggled to take in more than it could handle. What should they wear? Would people even come? How would I find the time to do it all—bake cookies, organize how they'd read, make time for more rehearsals? John tried to comfort me, tell me it would be okay, but I couldn't hear him through the noise of my anxiety.

I went down to Touchstone for an extra day the following week, ostensibly to rehearse. But we ended up spending most of the group time on an issue Lesley had brought up after we'd gathered. She told me Hiram had said at a staff meeting that all the girls do in our poetry group is sit around.

I was wild, a real banshee.

"Sharon, look at you, you are so upset. You know that's not true, we all work hard here. The staff doesn't understand anything anyway," Nadia tried to comfort me, seeing that I was almost in tears, clenching my fists.

"I am furious at him for saying that. It was thoughtless and cruel and completely wrong. The community doesn't seem to support our group and our reading. What can we do?"

Lesley's report had been a tipping point; all the stress I'd been under threatened to capsize me and our fragile program.

"Let's read our work to him tonight," Mayra said. "We'll do a confrontation."

The other girls and Lesley thought that was a great idea. But I was worried that it could further alienate the staff—I was also worried that they could interfere with our poetry group, claiming it wasn't within the "mission" and that letting the girls swear was all wrong. At least I knew that Lori was behind the program, and Lesley too, of course.

On the way home I tried to articulate to myself exactly what it was that I wanted from this Artwell performance. Okay, I mused, I wanted the girls to be heard, really heard, I wanted them to be queens for a night, to see and feel how their writing affected people, inspired people. I wanted whatever came.

Didn't I?

"Don't be too attached to outcomes," the Buddhist dharma whispered.

But I hungered for success.

We're on TV

I pulled into the parking lot, hands clenched on the steering wheel, and saw Lesley in the van with all the girls, ready to go. They were singing loudly, rocking back and forth in their seats to the music. Tiffany had never gotten parental permission, so she was unable to join us, nor was Isabella. Two of our strongest poets, damn. I was definitely too attached to outcomes.

We drove to the small cable TV studio in Torrington and rushed in; the girls wanted to adjust their makeup and hair before going on.

"My pimples!" Nia moaned.

"Can't even see them, Nia. Come on, Brian wants us to start."

Brian Judd, the talk show host, was kind to them, which made everything go easily. He took over, so I could sit back and watch. I was nervous about the profanity, but he seemed unfazed by it. The girls read Tiffany's and Isabella's poems in addition to their own, so Tiffany's abuser was actually named on the air.

Brian interviewed me for the first segment. I'd worn a blazer and a slim gray flannel skirt, wanting to look professional, grown-up, which I often never felt. Watching the video after the taping was over, I had a small epiphany. Viewing it, I was surprised by my authority and confidence in discussing the poetry project I'd brought into being at Touchstone; I actually experienced myself the way I'd tried to look.

The girls danced to rap in the parking lot and I joined in, exultant with our success. I took them all to Rossini's again for dinner, large pizzas, wings.

"Can you make one half-vegetarian?" I asked the waiter.

"Oh, I'm on a diet, Sharon, I'll have what you're having," Mayra said, nibbling on celery while the others gobbled their wings.

We'd picked up Isabella and Tiffany after the show. Isabella said little, and ate five pieces of sausage pizza in rapid succession.

"Sharon, I think you are letting us manipulate you into taking us out," Nia said.

"Whaaaat??" I said, truly stunned.

"Well, I have no problem letting my boyfriend pay, but I don't think you want to."

"Nia, I have no idea why you are saying that. I love being with all of you, I have money, and it gives me enormous pleasure to treat you, especially when you are locked up at Touchstone. This is fun for me."

None of them looked convinced. "Let go," I told myself again. I realized that they were not used to being given to, or even feeling they were worth being given to, and when anyone did offer something, they may have felt it was "give to get," that they now owed that person a debt.

Tiffany sat quietly next to me, eating slowly, elegantly. She carefully pondered the dessert menu and decided on New York cheesecake, which Nadia had too.

"What's your name?" Nia asked the waitress, the same one we'd had the last time.

"Clare." She smiled at the girls this time, and was kind. "Where're you young ladies from?" she wanted to know.

"Oh, we're from Touchstone. It's a boarding school in Litchfield."

Too much!

After Geoff died, I'd wanted to be with his friends all the time. I'd felt undefined, amorphous, with no clear boundaries or identity, not like a grown-up adult. I think I wanted to be one of them, as a way to be closer to him. And perhaps grief had reduced me, made me into a child again.

Now, though I was with these kids constantly, I was gratified to be an adult, to have choices, money, talent, a different life, to share with them. They wouldn't allow me to try to collapse generational boundaries. They wouldn't let me merge into their lives, as Geoff's friends willingly had. I couldn't control them or be a therapist or a teacher in our group. They usually nixed my suggestions for changes in their poems, defending their words with a passion that defied question.

But they allowed me to be a self with them I hadn't ever experienced, to explore what that self was, in ways I couldn't otherwise have encountered.

They were prying open my unwilling heart, helping me to imagine acceptance rather than rejection.

They were so tough, yet so vulnerable.

I was so tough, yet so vulnerable.

They were so scarred.

I was so scarred.

Heading back to Lakeville, I thought of what kindness, simple kindness, could do.

What's Love Got to Do with It?

I'd been in touch with a reporter from the *Waterbury Republican*, who had agreed to interview us for more Artwell publicity. On a spring afternoon in late May, we met down by the pond behind the big house. The girls clustered close together on a bench while I settled on the grass.

"Don't sit on the grass, Sharon!" Mayra yelled at me. "Bugs!"

I laughed. "Mayra, you are a city girl. I love to sit on grass. Bugs don't bother me." Ironically, they were all terrified of bugs, bears, deer, all the wildlife on Touchstone's fifty-seven acres, while my terror would be tapped by the drive-bys, drug dealing, and crime of their neighborhoods.

The reporter, a pleasant, earnest woman, worked hard at writing down everything the girls said, though cautioning them that all of it would not be in the article she wrote. They were hungry to be heard, and words spewed from them for the hour she stayed.

Isabella was not with us; Lesley said she had been in a time-out much of the day for head-banging. There was so much pain in that poor traumatized head of hers, maybe she'd just been trying to get it out.

Tiffany and Nadia had to leave for clinical sessions soon after the reporter did, but Nia, Mayra and Lesley lingered. The sun was warm, and none of us wanted to move.

"Sharon, how do you know if a man really loves you?" Nia wanted to know.

"Wow, Nia, that is a big question. If you say no to sex and it's okay with him, that would be a start. Sex should be just a part of the relationship, not all of it."

I told her I thought he needed to see you as an equal, respect you and your wants and needs as much as his own. You'd know, I said, as challenges came up in a long-term relationship, by how they got resolved—he'd be willing to negotiate with you so you both got something of what you wanted, not just you, not just him.

Nia gave me a blank look. I supposed I was giving much more information than had been asked for, and decided to stop while I was ahead.

"My boyfriend wants sex every day, but we do other things, like wrestling with each other," Mayra offered.

"I had a boyfriend who had another girlfriend who used to call while we were together." Nia told us.

"Did he talk to her?"

"Oh yes, Sharon!"

"Well, I would say that is definitely not a guy who really loves you."

We spoke of things boyfriends could do for girlfriends, tender, solicitous things.

"My boyfriend has written me every day since I've been here," Mayra said. "I think he's been faithful, but I don't know for sure. I would cut him off in a minute if I found out he hadn't been."

Nia's boyfriend was in jail.

So much of the writing and talking in poetry group revolved around love, what it was, what it wasn't, how to get it, keep it, how it felt to lose it, how it couldn't be trusted even though it was the most longed-for commodity in everyone's lives, including my own. There were questions always about who we wanted to love us—who we loved—drug-abusing mothers, absent fathers, alcoholic boyfriends, other residents, girlfriends, teachers, pets.

We all felt such a gut hunger to fill the huge holes childhood had left in us.

We were joined in this way, the girls and me. As the years of my work at Touchstone stretched ahead, I would find this fact a constant kick behind the knees, a truth of my life I hadn't wanted to embrace. I had thought all the years of therapy training and personal therapy, so much living through grief and loss, had more or less healed me.

I was wrong.

There had been little warmth or affection in my family of origin. My mother had apologized for that, but her regret didn't remove the ravenous need from the little girl she never held or hugged. My own father never once said he loved me, and had been mostly absent from my life, except for the frequent abusive criticism he generously doled out and his reluctant presence at the family holiday dinners I hosted at my home. Yes, he'd given me cars and money, but never an embrace.

I really got it, in my guts, what the girls struggled with, the empty places that yearned for fullness, the fruitless relationships we all sought with impoverished lovers and friends in a compulsive repetition of our pasts. No theoretical learning, this.

"Let's write about love," I suggested. We all picked up our notebooks.

The girls are full of words about love. It's on their minds. It's on everyone's minds. "I want love. I need love" Sometimes what that means is that I want to be the center of someone else's world, no matter who that person is—I just want what they have to give me.

Sometimes, it's just lust. I want you. I feel the quivering in my genitals. Sexual attraction. Easy to be confused, easy to confuse this for love. People will do a lot to satisfy their lust. You all know what guys will do early in a relationship. They'll say anything to get into your pants, right? Now that there are so many girl-girl relationships, the same thing probably happens. Gender equality, I guess.

Real love. Now that's something else. There's the love of mother for child, child for parent, sister for sister, sister for brother, and so on. These loves are non-erotic. And should be. A serious boundary is crossed when a sibling or parent acts out sexually with a child. These are supposed to be safe relationships, relationships you can trust. Parental love should offer guidance, help, support, attention to who you really are, not who Mom and Dad want you to be. It should help you find ways to become that person. Parents are supposed to be responsible—food, clothing, shelter, education—to fill their child's needs for touch, deep connection.

What are a child's responsibilities to a parent? I guess you could say respect, but a parent needs to earn it, in my opinion. My father always insisted on respect, but I didn't respect him. I couldn't, seeing the way he treated me, my sisters, and my mother. A child owes her parent something, though. Listening, I guess, paying attention, gratitude—but only if the parent deserves it, if parents walk their talk, do their job. In my mind parents owe their children more than children owe their parents. A child doesn't ask to be born.

I Am Not a Juvenile Delinquent

137

Then there's the big love—relationship love, committed love. Maybe married love. Of course it all starts with attraction— falling in love. Then being in love. Many who theorize about this subject say that a love relationship generally survives maybe two years before disillusionment sets in. Persons in a couple are initially attracted to each other for their differences—the qualities that he/she didn't possess—"opposites attract"—but now they each burned with the frustrating question of why the other couldn't be more like him or her. If the relationship was to grow into a mature one, a long-term commitment, much work necessarily began here.

There is something different that comes with the "feeling" of love to me that is shown in action, not words. It's faith, loyalty, trust, kindness. Integrity, companionship. Shared values, the willingness to work through conflicts and the acquisition of knowledge of how to do that. Would you trust this person with your life? That's pretty big. And a good question to ask yourself about someone who says he or she loves you.

I was so grateful to have the husband I'd had for forty-eight years. Despite the void I carried from my childhood, from the death of my son, from my array of failed relationships with others, I had this bedrock man. There were still struggles and challenges in our long "out of the box" marriage, but I could rest with him, feel accepted and safe. And I had my children, my love for the dead son as great as that for the living one. And now my three grandchildren.

I wanted the girls to know that some love can last.

Artwell

I'd been on an island in Maine for the Memorial Day weekend. For the whole celebratory time with friends and family, all that had been on my mind was Artwell, as the June 1 date grew closer. I'd made up a program which they immediately demanded to have changed, wanting to read poems different from what I'd chosen. Tiffany insisted I retype her poems exactly as she had written them. I was really worried about all the "bitches and niggas," and I was right to be, as I would soon discover.

At our next meeting, Lesley was off, so we had Angel, and on top of that disruption we had to meet in that cold, dark living room. The gurgles of the fish tank made their already too-soft voices impossible to hear, so I pulled the plug.

They read horribly.

"I'll keep time, Sharon," Isabella assured me, so I gave her the kitchen timer I'd brought along. But there were so many interruptions that her job became impossible. Other staff walked in and out of the room. A group of residents marched through to get to the adjoining "library," so called due to the two or three shelves of outdated books it held. Angel's walkie-talkie seemed particularly active today, spewing out counts every ten minutes. Nia held the poems over her face and was laughing as she read.

"I think you enjoy swearing, Nia," Angel interjected.

Tiffany wanted to show me a new poem she'd been working on.

Alone Again

Alone again
No one to hug or hold me
Alone again
No one to show they love me
Alone again

Dying in the corner
Alone again
When my heart feels murdered
Alone again
No one to speak or hear me
Alone again
No one to steer me
Alone again
I feel nobody knows me
Alone again
A victim of society
Do you hear my cry?
Alone again
I don't have to hide
Alone again
No one even sees me
Alone again
Walk over me like feces
Alone again
No one to hug or hold me
Alone again
No one to show they love me

"That's fantastic, Tiffany. Do you want to read that one too?"

"I'm not sure yet, Sharon."

The next time we all met would be at Artwell. We'd just have to wing it.

●　●　●

The night before the big night, I got a call from Lori. A few of the staff had seen the TV show and had been outraged at the profanity, especially in Nadia's poems. I'd suspected that this was coming. I was terrified that she'd cancel the show. This was a challenge for her, I knew. She supported me, the project, and the girls, but politics and bad language were issues that she, as Touchstone's director, couldn't ignore.

"Sharon, what do you think about just going through the poems and taking out a lot of the offensive words?"

I tried to find the positive in this new crisis, took some long, deep breaths, pondered what the Buddhist dharma would tell me here.

"Let's go through them, okay?"

"Will you show them to the girls after we've fixed them? I don't know how it will go over, they are so protective of their words."

"They'll be okay, Sharon. I'll work with them on it, explain."

We interrogated each of the poems they'd be reading, and were able to keep their integrity despite the pruning.

"But 'niggas' has to stay." She was okay with that.

"I'm afraid my boss will be coming, and she would be very upset to hear all that language."

Lori and I reached a compromise easily, and I thought the poems were made much stronger by the culling. It was so much better that she had done it and not me, I thought. She called me the next morning, the day of the performance, and said they'd been fine with it all, they'd understood.

So the show would go on.

●　●　●

I arrived an hour early at the gallery on Water Street with the batch of oatmeal cookies I'd made for the audience, some rice and broccoli for my supper, and five red roses in a large white box. I found a place to hide the box so I could surprise the girls at the end of the show. I'd also brought some big jugs of soda for the guests, as well as six-packs of Dr. Pepper and Sprite for the girls.

Stewart Wilson, the gallery director, had given me the combination to get the door open. Once in, I stood for a while in the empty space, wondering would happen there tonight. It was a humble room, almost shabby—a storefront, in a blue-collar town. No chairs, tables, podium or mike, either. Just some amateurish art on the walls.

The friend who'd offered to help me arrived soon after I did, and we dragged chairs up from the basement, located a big table for the refreshments. She found the mike and organized its installation competently. We unearthed a white sculpture stand to serve as a podium.

Now all we needed was the girls.

And suddenly here they were, blazing through the door right on time, looking gorgeous in long skirts and high-heeled shoes, those ersatz nail extensions, full makeup. They were excited, yet unsure, now far from their comfort zone.

Lori and Lesley had brought them. Lori had gotten carnation corsages for everyone and we pinned them on. I exclaimed over how beautiful they looked. They approved of my outfit too, a long black skirt and sleeveless white top, my collection of silver bangles. There was a corsage for me as well; I stuck myself with the hatpin trying to fasten it to my top.

"Mayra, can you help me with this?"

"Sure I can, Sharon."

"We're hungry, Sharon. We didn't have dinner."

"Lesley, can you go out and find them some pizza? I think there's a place up the street. Here's some cash." I handed her a twenty-dollar bill. "Is that enough?"

"Sure, Sharon, no problem! I know a place. I'll be back as fast as I can."

Stewart arrived and brought up the rest of the chairs, but then suggested that we put some of them away so it wouldn't look empty if not a lot of people showed up.

"No, Stewart, I think we should leave them."

Actually, I was afraid he was right. But then, if he wasn't, we'd have to drag them all back up. Too much trouble.

My friend was working with the girls on the mike, and what a difference it was making. I could finally really hear them, and they loved using it, lifted out of its slot on the stand. Tiffany was especialy poised. She planned to read her abuse poem tonight, herself.

Lesley arrived with the pizza and the girls went to a back room to eat.

People began to arrive. A lot of Touchstone staff and other girls. Others started pouring in. A whole bunch of my friends, one who'd driven all the way from Cape Cod, the poetry group I belonged to. Lots of people I didn't even know. The girls were charged now, working the crowd, acting

Artwell

like stars. I was feeling almost faint with exhilaration and amazement, and probably hunger, as I'd totally forgotten my broccoli and rice.

All the chairs had quickly filled. It was a hot night and people began to fan themselves. I was afraid the heat might make them leave, but already people were standing outside. Nadia was looking anxiously for her mother, who had promised to come. My husband arrived, some of my clients.

The audience I'd wanted for my girls was more than here, overflowing.

I took a deep breath, thanked everyone profusely, and made the remarks I'd prepared.

> *I believe we live in a world that is in a general state of denial—a world that works hard at sanitizing life and presenting it to us on the news, in the other media, as reality. It's not. There is a kind of holocaust going on today in the lives of many teenagers; you will hear of that holocaust tonight in language that may jolt you, in language that is not that of either dead white males or middle-class white females. It is Mayra's language, Nia's language, Nadia's language, Isabella's language, Tiffany's language. It is the language necessary to tell what it tells. These young women are courageous and gutsy, wise beyond their years. In sharing their stories and poems with you, they are making themselves vulnerable in ways that most of us would never dream of. Since there is no one to speak for them, they are speaking for themselves. Their voices come directly from the dangerous back roads of their hearts, and tell you of their journeys to the edge and back. I am thrilled to present them to you.*

Tiffany began with *Speak*. She was her usual fashion-queen self, with heels so high she had even more presence than usual.

Mayra followed with the poignant letter to her mother she'd written, so full of pain, abandonment, and agonized questions (in an earlier chapter).

To me, her letter captured the essence of why so many of the girls were here. When I looked out over the audience, I saw people were mesmerized.

Isabella read *It's Reality*. I saw people wiping away tears.

Nadia's mother had arrived late, but she was here, with Nadia's three brothers.

During the intermission, Stewart had door prizes and let the girls award them. Another friend was taking pictures, and many more came up to me with tears in their eyes to tell me they'd never heard anything like this. My husband held me in a huge hug. We got another invitation to do a radio show, someone from Connecticut Junior Republic (a disciplinary facility for boys) wanted to know how to do a poetry program there, and someone else wanted the girls to become involved in an Empowering Women Project. She said she'd be in touch.

I couldn't remember when I'd been this happy.

The second half of the reading was even better than the first. Tiffany's poems were especially stunning.

Won't You Be My Medicine?

Won't you be my medicine?
Make me feel all better inside?
Don't allow my feelings to hide.
Don't allow my tears to cry.
Shelter my heart so it won't feel alone.
Bring my thoughts to reality.
Show me someone who unconditionally loves me.

Won't you be my medicine?
Someone to understand my reality—
undo my discouragement—
hand me knowledge and strength to grow
and regardless of what happens
allow my pride to continue standing tall.

Won't you be my medicine?
So you can make my anger go away—
Don't allow it to turn to hate.

Just please be my medicine
So my heart can be pure and sweet.
When it's not full of love it's incomplete.
I need a teaspoon of medicine to keep
me going in life, allow me to progress—

Artwell

steer me away from dimness to the positive light.

Let me learn from my mistakes.
Just destroy my hate, and be
my permanent medicine inside
so my cold won't turn into my personal mate.
Oh, medicine. I love you!
Do you know what medicine I take?

The applause never seemed to end. I gave each of the girls a rose and a huge hug, and they surprised me with a big bouquet of flowers. Each girl spoke.

I began to cry.

"Sharon gives us her personal time, and we really appreciate that," Nia told the audience. "She doesn't even get paid to be with us."

"If it weren't for Sharon, I'd never be writing," Nadia informed us, her mother and brothers looking on with enormous pride.

And then it was over. I stayed to help clean up, savoring every minute of the still-hot June night. I was sure the girls had gotten something that would find its way into their limbic systems, nudge their trauma into a corner, for tonight, at least.

Still high with the evening when I got home, I put the flowers in a vase, had a glass of wine with my proud husband, and went up to my study to write to them.

> *My dearest girls,*
>
> *What a night! What a performance! You should be so proud of yourselves. I know you are. I know I surely am. I want you to carry this night with you forever. In dark times, remember the night you reached the hearts of all of those people with your words, remember their hushed awe, their amazement, their thrilling applause. You've made your short lives into art; you've transformed pain and suffering into poetry that in turn has reached others and transformed them. There is no higher calling for a writer. You are all writers now; you must keep on writing, it has become your calling. Words matter—you know*

that now, truly. You have developed the gift to shape language into meaning—to name things—to pull the dark shadows from the corners of your souls and bring them into the light. This is true power.

I have arranged your beautiful flowers and put them up here next to my computer so I can see them as I write this letter. That seems fitting! Your words to me last night meant more than I can say. I felt bathed in love and appreciation. I felt the joy of a teacher who knows her lessons have been absorbed. I felt a love stirrring in me that I haven't felt since before my son died. There is a hole in my heart that is being filled. Thank you for this. There is no more that you could give me.

Enjoy the afterglow of the night. It was a true triumph, and what made it so was that you were simply yourselves, proud, strong, and beautiful black queens. I hope you will write something about your experience and bring it the next time we meet.

> *With much love and appreciation,*
> *Sharon*

The next morning I faxed it to Lori, who promised me she'd give each girl a copy.

Everyone at Touchstone, at least those with whom she had spoken, had given positive feedback.

"Sharon, it was wonderful. A great night. Thank you so much."

And, to my utter surprise, was I ever in let-down mode.

A Scar Unraveling

"May I be peaceful, may I be happy, may I be safe, may I be free."

I wanted that, I really did. That's what I told myself anyway, as I spoke these Buddhist loving-kindness phrases over and over again, longing for the release they could bring. I'd been at Touchstone for ten months now, shaping the poetry program as an enthused initiate. But for the next year, I was a scar unraveling. If that first group had been the curative, falling-in-love phase of a relationship, scarring over my grief, this next part was the disillusionment phase.

It was hard for new groups to coalesce. When girls left, there was major disruption and acting out.

And worse, when I welcomed the new girls with warmth, the old ones pulled back silent and distant. It took me time to realize that they were feeling loss, perhaps even betrayal. I had belonged to them, and now they were jealous as I became symbolic mother, teacher, lover, friend, and mentor to these new creative writing members.

I wrestled constantly with the planning and organizing of our field trips. Always, they provoked chaos. I repeatedly questioned the wisdom of continuing to add these outside readings and events, but then the events were always so rewarding, I'd quickly plan another.

I'd be self-critical—"Sharon, you're just too lazy to keep trying. You know it's hard, but just push through. Deal with the stress. Look at the value for the girls."

I developed tendonitis in my right arm from all the typing of their poems. I wondered whether I was too old for this work. My poetry friends admonished me that this job left little time for my own writing. Much of the staff continued to oppose my outings and meetings. When I came home from our sessions ready to drop, my husband, though he knew how I cherished the girls and the work, would ask why I continued to do it if it stressed and discouraged me so much.

Nadia and Tiffany had a graduation ceremony at which they profusely thanked everyone at Touchstone who had helped them but me. I was crushed, and embarrassed by my feelings. Isabella, who stayed on for many more months, became chronically suicidal and generally unstable—she'd told me her mother didn't care if she committed suicide—and was only sporadically able to be at our meetings. She continued to write stunning poems, however.

A bunch of new residents came and went; some flourished in the group; many were static. Lesley was a constant support, though, as was Lori. Sometimes the girls tried to manipulate me, and I worked ceaselessly for a balance between good boundaries and compassion, for control and giving up control.

But I persevered.

Into this maelstrom came Tarray, Chimere, and Jeni, three unusually strong, bright, and gifted young women.

Tarray

This girl was tough, funny, confident, talented. And smart, smarter than most of the staff at Touchstone. Tarray provided a vexing challenge to all of us, but I had the optimal circumstances in which to experience the best of her, with the poetry program she came to love.

I don't remember why she'd been sent to Touchstone, but whatever her charges had been, she'd done a lot worse. Tarray's grandmother Cecile, a fine churchgoing lady, had become her guardian while her parents were in jail.

Tarray was openly gay, and her grandmother couldn't accept that.

I tried to talk with her about it, but Cecile didn't want to deal with this at all. All she wanted was for Tarray to wear feminine clothes, finish high school, and go to a good college.

Tarray was an imposing presence, tall and weighty. She favored Ralph Lauren men's shorts and shirts, Timberland boots, expensive sneakers, baseball caps. She had such a commanding personality that staff were actually afraid of her.

She'd been awarded a basketball scholarship to the elite Miss Porter's School in Farmington and had turned it down.

I'd had trouble believing that when I'd heard it—why would anyone turn down a scholarship to a prestigious private school? It took me a long time to process the lessons my crusade for Tarray would provide—the crusade for her to have the life I was sure she could have, the one her grandmother wanted for her.

She was tight with Chimere, who had been her best friend since middle school, and Ellie, a flinty Caucasian girl who wore a headscarf and had converted to Islam in her first lock-up. Ellie was the best rapper I'd ever heard. These three residents loved my group, the only thing at Touchstone that interested them. It provided an activity at which they excelled.

Buoyed by this new poetic dynamite, I'd felt rejuvenated and recommitted to doing the weekly sessions. And their enthusiasm energized the rest of the group. Tuesday afternoons were transformed.

Stewart Wilson had invited us back for another Artwell reading (and continued to for the ten years I was there), and that year's was probably the most powerful performance we'd ever do. The girls were prepared, excited, even rehearsed on their own. But the day before, Ellie was told she couldn't participate because she had reputedly made an anti-Semitic remark to another girl. It was hard for me to believe this for several reasons: she'd never done anything like that before, was generally respectful and kept to herself, and sometimes girls accused other girls of doing things because of spite or jealousy.

And I cared for her so much, I didn't want to believe it.

As a punishment, or "consequence" as it was called at Touchstone, she was put on TBS (trust-building status). Her room was emptied of everything; all privileges were removed.

We'd planned that she and Tarray would open the reading with a sensational original rap—no one else could possibly have taken their place.

Michelle, the new program director, would not relent and let Ellie come.

I questioned her sources, the evidence, pleaded that she be allowed to perform with us. Ellie absolutely denied making the remark, but Michelle and the clinical director stood firm.

I ached for Ellie, and brought a rose to her empty room the next day. Despite the fact that the situation had created unnecessary pain and disorder for all of us, it was still a stellar show.

Tarray, in dark glasses and a bright red T-shirt, read compelling poems, as did Chimere and the other girls who performed that night.

This one, Tarray's, was done to a prompt I would use many times over, as it evoked such strong responses in the girls, some of whom did not even have a kitchen table but yearned for its symbolic comfort.

Tarray

My Kitchen Table

my kitchen table is the hangout.
we don't eat there but we express ourselves there
How many kids does so and so have?
How many times have the bill collectors called?
How much is the phone bill?
that's the food on my kitchen table
we eat the gossip in the air
we eat our wisdom at the kitchen table
not the wisdom of books and school
but the wisdom of the projects,
welfare dick, fast cars, drug money—
our kitchen table is as well-rounded
as if the Mafia were there
fuck my kitchen table
there's nothing there to eat
I've been eating the same shit there forever
I want different foods at my kitchen table
no gossip or shit from the streets
I want the food of books and school
how to make it
I want to digest the food at my kitchen table
let it move through my system
return again at the table
fuck the food at the projects, welfare dick,
fast cars and drug money
I want some new food at my kitchen table

On the advice of a poet friend, I sent some of Tarray's poems to a Connecticut high school competition, Fresh Voices, sponsored by the Hill-Stead Museum in Farmington. She was one of the winners, and the only person of color in the group of seven. The others were privileged white kids from private schools and the Hartford Academy, a special magnet school for the gifted.

The *Hartford Courant* ran an article with a big photo. It was thrilling. Or at least I was thrilled. I didn't know about Tarray. As usual, she affected nonchalance, but I knew she had to be happy, at least about the prospect of getting out of Touchstone for all the practice readings and meetings we would have to attend.

I worried that she wouldn't take this enormous honor seriously enough and keep her nose clean so she could stay on level and be transported to all the events, as the staff would be responsible for taking her while she was still incarcerated. I was concerned that Touchstone wouldn't take it seriously enough, either. I thought she might just impulsively decide not to participate one day and that I'd never be able to talk her back into it. I agonized about the real possibility of staff and peer backlash, jealousy, and sabotage. I wondered how she'd get along with the other winners. I was anxious about what she would wear. And I was right to worry. Much went smoothly, but much did not.

Fortunately, Tarray had the strong backing of her grandmother, who saw how important this experience could be for her future and supported her all the way. But after she was discharged, she moved in with her grandfather, who lived in an iffy area of Hartford. She could get to the practice readings that preceded the big festival, but there was no way for her to get home unless I took her.

I dreaded driving Tarray back to her dangerous neighborhood. My sister was horrified when I told her where I was going at night in my black Saab. "They have drive-by shootings there, Sharon!" And Tarray herself told me I wasn't safe alone. But since she wouldn't be able to get home any other way, I kept doing it, heart pounding out of my chest after I dropped her off. With her in the car, though, I felt safe.

The evening fulfilled every promise. The exquisite sunken gardens at the Hill-Stead were in full bloom. The weather was perfect, and there was an audience of at least 1500 sitting on blankets and lawn chairs. Two gifted young performers played cello and violin as an opener for the reading. The other kids were excellent, but Tarray was the star. Not only could she write well, she knew how to deliver a performance. Denise thought she sounded like Bessie Smith, the great jazz and blues singer. You had to be there, really to hear the melody, depth, and rhythm in her voice.

Smooth Pain

my pain you can't touch
it's untouchable
even I can't touch it
I can only feel it
it's a smooth feeling
smoother than a baby's ass
smoother than teddy pendergrass
yes, but pain
pain when I walk
pain when I move
just smooth pain
sometimes people say
pain will heal
mine hasn't yet
it feels like the pain
my ancestors went through
it feels like the pain of a starving child
in the middle of the street
the pain of an old man robbed
of everything even his socks
the pain of the world
more pain
less pain
smooth pain

Tarray stood there in her shorts and shirt looking like she had been born to the spotlight—not happy, exactly, but confident and strong. The applause was enormous. I sobbed, my husband's proud arm tight around my shoulder. Her jubilant grandmother, grandfather, and brother stood next to me. Farmington, Avon, and West Hartford adults and kids, adoring parents and relatives of the other performers, surrounded us with praise and accolades.

Now I thought that she could move with ease into the wider world, the world of scholarship and accomplishment, which she would, after this, want to. Right?

After one of the practice readings, Pam Nomura, Denise Abercrombie, the mentor given her for the win, and I had begun talking. Pam was the director of creative writing at the Hartford Academy, a magnet school for gifted kids in Hartford with special afternoon arts classes in the afternoon for kids from other districts. Tarray would be perfect there, we all thought. It was a school with lots of creative, dramatic kids like her, lots of opportunities to use and train her talent for performance poetry. Living again with her grandmother, she'd be going back to South Windsor High after Touchstone and could be bused in after her regular morning scheduled classes.

Her grandparents were completely for it. Denise and I wrote long recommendations, assuring all who would read them that Tarray would and could succeed at this wonderful school, that it would give her the opportunities she so needed. Pam was able to get scholarship money from an anonymous donor.

We were all so proud of ourselves.

Grandmother Cecile was exultant and bought Tarray lots of great new clothes. I spoke to the social worker at her school in South Windsor. I spoke to her parole officer. Finally we all met and talked with Tarray and asked if she was really up for this.

"Yeah, sure," she said.

We thought we'd covered it all.

In September I went on a long-planned three-week trip to Italy with my husband. I had talked with Tarray before I left and everything had seemed fine, settled, although she wasn't as excited about the Academy as I wished she were. When I returned, there was an email from Pam.

> We need to meet, Sharon. Tarray isn't showing up for classes. Get her grandparents in and let's all talk about it.

We had the meeting. Pam presented the issues compassionately but firmly. Her grandparents seemed nonplussed. Tarray just shrugged her shoulders and said she'd try harder to go to class. I took her out for dinner after the meeting at a nearby restaurant.

"What's up, girl? Why aren't you going to classes? They're so perfect for you, performance poetry, poetry writing, the other kids seem really talented, the school is gorgeous, state-of-the-art everything. I don't understand. It's not like you're locked up there."

"I don't know, Sharon." She looked down at the table, anywhere but into my eyes. She didn't have an answer. But she told me about the demands of the two girlfriends she was juggling, neither of whom knew about each other.

"One is a bad girl, she's gorgeous—we go to clubs; the other a good girl— she goes to college and wants me to go too. I'm always caught between these types, Sharon."

"Are you back on drugs? Selling? Using?"

"Nope. But I hate South Windsor—didn't start on time anyway. We didn't get the registration paperwork in when they wanted it. The social worker there is a bitch, Sharon."

She said she'd try to go to class.

We met again. And again. She was failing everything due to non-attendance. She had to leave. No more scholarship, no more chances. She didn't seem to care.

I was the one who'd cared.

Tarray had had me as secretary in creative writing, typing all her poems. She'd come each week because it was the only thing that interested her. And, locked up, she couldn't leave Touchstone or blow it off, so she chose to attend creative writing rather than sit in her room planning escapes or conquests. At the Academy, she'd been forced to work, show up for classes and write papers, be responsible, fulfill its high standards.

But Tarray wanted the freedom of the clubs, the streets, of the bad girl.

In her backwards baseball cap and baggy shorts, she was my perfect Buddhist teacher, a whole PhD program in the dangers of attachment, the certainty of impermanence, the folly of desiring things to be other than how they are.

Chimere

Chimere was electric. From the first time I met her, I felt her vitality, her vividness. She was different from the other residents—not a fighter, or aggressive. Chimere had a positive attitude about life. She cared about the needs of others, and was kind, unusual for Touchstone girls.

Chimere was beautiful, and wore outfits that enhanced her attractiveness—matching pink Coach leather belts and bags, classy tops with the tight jeans that all the girls wore, only they always looked better on her, somehow. She unfailingly had a French tip manicure, and her hair seemed to change style and color every week. Clearly her family was better off financially than those of the other girls; she'd evidently had a lawyer to keep her out of York CI, the Connecticut prison for women, though she told me her charge had only been for fighting another girl.

At one of our sessions, Chimere had written about being in the wrong place at the wrong time—the back seat of a stolen car, a joy ride, a boy driving it who had killed its owner. The police had stopped and searched the car, finding contraband in the trunk. She and the other kid in the backseat had been ordered to lie flat on the ground. The driver and his accomplice went to jail. Fortunately, they let Chimere and the boy go.

It had taken her a while to join the poetry group—she told me she'd had difficulty trusting anyone at Touchstone. She knew she'd have to risk trust to join our group. But when she finally decided to, she gave it her all.

There was a passion in her poems, a rhythm and cadence, an honesty of heart. Her voice was mellifluous, and hearing her read was a treat. She took the group seriously, and brought us all to a higher level. The wrangling and struggling ceased, for the most part, when Chimere was present. Her long friendship with Tarray made them a strong twosome, and along with Ellie, they gave our group a gravitas it wouldn't have had otherwise.

In one of her early poems, confidence blooms through her struggles.

No More Heavy Rains

If I could turn the hands of time around I would—
not ashamed to say I'm ugly, dumb, crazy, just nothing—
No, I am smart, beautiful, in control
I am something.
Those days that thundered on me, poured rain,
flooded me with hate
finally let the sun shine on me—
my flowers blossomed, did yours?
You always gotta struggle to get to the top
life's too short, why can't I live forever?
Why, can I ask you?
Let me know why I am here—
why I am miserable—no, maybe depressed—
oh no, I got it, stressed—
because I'd like thunder on me
rain pouring on me
flooding me in darkness—

Sunshine, sunshine, oh yes here you are—
yes, I am someone
you've brightened my skies
There's no thunder, no heavy rain
there's light
I'm not ugly
I'm not dumb
I'm not crazy
I'm not just anything
I am Chimere

Life's too short to be in darkness
I am the sunshine that brings the light.

Chimere had been committed to Touchstone for a year, a pretty long stint. She had read beautifully at Artwell—some of her family members had come, and she had been dazzling in a shimmery dress with a matching coat-jacket, looking like the lady she saw herself as.

I Am Not a Juvenile Delinquent

I remember standing in the dining room, just before she was due to be discharged. Chimere's assigned chore for that evening was to sweep the dreary room; she leaned on the broom and looked at me hopefully, asking if we could stay in touch.

"Sharon, when I get out, do you think it would be okay to call you sometime, you know, when things get tough and I need support?"

"Of course, Chimere," I quickly said. "I would love that." I gave all the girls my number when they left and encouraged them to use it any time.

And she had stayed in touch. Phone calls, mostly. We've had lunch many times through the eighteen years since we'd met at Touchstone. She'd returned as an "alumna reader" with Tarray for the poetry festivals I planned each summer, and some Artwell readings. She always said, "I love you, Sharon," at the end of our conversations, and then would ask to be remembered to John, my husband.

I'd always been eager to follow her pregnancies, the first one in 2005, with Muhlanie. Now she was pregnant for the third time, and we planned to meet at Bar Taco in West Hartford for lunch to catch up.

When we spotted each other, we quickly fell into a long hug.

"Let's go sit down, I got a booth for us," I said.

Being six months along, it was a tricky maneuver to squeeze into the booth for her, her big red brass-zippered Steve Madden bag and her puffy pale pink coat adding to the pregnancy bulk. Chimere's black hair was long and gently curled. She wore a short-sleeved pink top over her swollen belly, a large pink and white flower-patterned shell necklace with pearl earrings. Her arms were loaded with tattoos.

I thought she was gorgeous.

We talked about Tarray, her grandmother's death, and how Tarray's life was still in chaos. We discussed the baby she wasn't sure she wanted, pregnant by a man who had let her down at every turn, but was her second child's father.

"After the baby comes, definitely, I will definitely send him packing."

"But won't it be harder then?"

The question hung in the air between us.

"Why do I get with these bad men?" she wondered aloud. "Was it because my father wasn't there for me?"

"They are attracted to you because you're smart, beautiful, steady, keep a lovely home, and have a profession." (Chimere is a dental assistant.) "They can feed off you, and you can feel good about yourself for being better than they are. Weird payoff. And sometimes good men are boring. No drama. And I know there's a big part of you that loves drama."

I told her my mother's story, of being engaged to a WASP Yale student who, according to her account anyway, adored her and to whom she was actually engaged. Then she met my father, an exciting, handsome, wild, and unattainable type, relentlessly chased him for five years until he proposed. And they ended up with a terrible marriage.

"You are such a wonderful mother," I said. "But you are too loyal sometimes to the wrong people. I know, I've been there too. People sometimes are attracted to me because they think I will help them."

"You are strong, Sharon."

"So are you, Chimere. We have to use our strengths to help ourselves first. That's a hard lesson, believe me, I know."

We made plans to meet before the baby came, maybe in May when I would be back from a trip to Italy. I had been so involved in our conversation that all notion of time had been suspended. As we put on our coats and hugged goodbye, I thought again how incredibly lucky I was to have these young women in my life. Being with them gives me something I can get nowhere else. They are real, we are real together, as real as real can get.

In our shared worlds, I become who I want to be, at least for a time, free from conflict, clear in vision, full of gratitude, touched by grace.

While I was writing this book, I told her she would be featured in a profile and that I'd love to know what our poetry sessions had been like for her. She quickly responded:

> Creative writing (that's what the girls called it) was a blessing for me. It was a place I went to that had other people there but I had my own place in creative writing. It brought me to another level, cleaned my open wounds, helped me sit back, relax and use my

I Am Not a Juvenile Delinquent

mind to its full potential. Creative writing has helped me inside and out. It gave me the opportunity to look deep into my life, and finally take control of it. It was and will always be a breath of fresh air. It helped me escape all unimportant things in life without being judged.

My relationship with you (Sharon) is like no other, the love I have for you is like no other. God has never shared someone so loving and forgiving, sweet, generous and outrageous as you are, Sharon. Sometimes I feel like giving up and every time I do you pop up in my life and make me realize what life is really worth living for. You are my inspiration, my joy, you believe in me, you tell me like it is, you stand by me, fight for me, Sharon you are my friend and it is a true honor to say that with confidence. Writing is so important because it helps you find yourself, helps you use your brain and think about what life prepares for us and how to handle it.

Writing will always be a part of my life. Since I have become a writer I have looked at so many things in such deep ways and it makes me feel a bit ahead. Writing is my life and what makes me who I am. You just have to be open to understand writing.

Chimere

Jeni

The trees were gleaming red and yellow in the most stunning fall spectacle I could remember. Riding down to Broad Brook from Lakeville, I thought they were celebrating the wedding to come with their wild, sun-shot color.

Determined to attend it, I had postponed needed back surgery so I could be there. Jeni and I had sustained a relationship over the time since the year she'd been at Touchstone. After Tarray and Chimere left, I'd been eager to have her in the new group.

It was a selfish desire. After I'd met her, I knew she'd be a serious, steadying ballast for the group, as they had been. She'd been at Steppingstone, a sister facility, for a year and had just arrived at Touchstone when I first asked her to join.

She said she'd think about it and let me know.

A few weeks later, impatient for her presence in the group, I asked her again. She'd said she still wasn't ready, but would let me know when she was. It took a few more months for her to make the commitment.

That deliberative manner of hers had followed her into adulthood. It took Jeni time to make important decisions, and she made them carefully.

But I could only wonder how she made the decision at age fourteen to become involved with an older man, drugs, and a succession of thefts in her community. Later Jeni told me that her status as a special child in her family had made her mother tremendously overprotective. She'd been grounded for months at a time because of bad grades, so she'd begun skipping school to have a social life with friends who did the same. Her delinquency was both wrenching and shocking to her mom and dad.

It was unusual for a middle-class Caucasian family to be "in the system," and though Jeni was angry and resistant for much of her incarceration, her parents unswervingly stood by her, paying huge lawyer's fees, visiting weekly, and willingly engaging in family therapy, which helped them to see their own roles in their special child's disastrous choices. Their participation, support, and constancy had a great deal to do with Jeni's successful transition to adulthood.

Jeni was a slim, quiet young woman whose pretty, clean-cut looks belied her crime. She always wore immaculate, tight, low-cut jeans with a stylish, attractive top. Her straight light brown hair fell into her eyes when she leaned toward me to read, and she would repeatedly brush it back, reciting her poems with intense concentration.

Jeni was earnest about creative writing. She was never disruptive or misbehaving, an excellent model for the rest of the girls in the group, who all respected her. And it made my job the joy that I'd longed for since being at Touchstone.

Nothing was hard with Jeni there.

But free-writing was tough for her. She used our workshop time to carefully craft poems despite my constant admonitions to just let her words flow. She crumpled up and threw many pages on the floor in anger or disgust.

They were poems that showed a deep desire to be understood, and to understand herself and others. Poems that explored the challenging relationships with both her parents. Poems that struggled with the pain and need to let go of the unhealthy relationship she'd had with the man who'd been her partner in crime, who was now incarcerated. Poems that dealt with all the conflict and anguish adolescents have around adults. Perceptive, thoughtful poems that I loved typing, each one better than the next.

The Door at the Top of the Stairs

When you turn that knob, what do you expect?
Can you see yourself in a mirror?
Is there a picture in your mind—or is it blank?
Is it a freeze-frame in time—are you stuck
with yourself, afraid of the unknown, where it's dark
and the only insight is your own imagination?
The only light, the whites of your eyes?

Jeni

Can you heal the selfish cries
that flee from your soul?
Are you more afraid of what's on the other side
Have you lost your better judgment

'cause something is pulling you near?
It's the fear that churns inside
that makes you feel complete—
you long to silence the suffering pain.
By standing in this stairway
you'll always be in the dark—
you'll always have that feeling
that drowns you deep inside
until you open that door
and it shows you where to begin
it all starts the healing within.

Slowly, Jeni gave up her angry resistance, and gained level five, the highest one achievable at Touchstone. Her parole was shortened and she was allowed to go home after two years, where she finished high school and settled into living the next part of her life.

She and I stayed in touch by phone, with email and visits. We became important people in each other's lives.

She discarded one relationship and job, then met Kyle, got another job at a bank, and started night school. Her life seemed to become steadier. Jeni brought Kyle up to meet me for lunch in a Lakeville restaurant; she'd thrust out her right hand to show me the ring.

Too soon, I thought, and *too young*. Wasn't there time?

I went to her wedding shower. It was a surprise for Jeni, and my being there was an even bigger surprise. There were many women in pretty summer dresses, much food and cake, a table full of gifts, the typical bridal shower. Pancake griddles and panini grills, the traditional bouquet of ribbons made by her maid of honor, games and champagne.

She walked me to the door when I left, telling me how much it meant to her that I had come, crying suddenly on my shoulder. Her mother walked with us, tearfully saying that without me, we all wouldn't be here today.

And I cried too, with grief over her past, euphoria that she had come so far.

The three of us shared a long hug.

And now, I was on my way to the wedding.

When the music started and Jeni came down the aisle on her dad's arm, more tears and memories deluged me. I'd been to many weddings. But this one was different. I knew the twisting loops of the journey that had brought this bride to this aisle.

She turned to look at me and grinned. Her soft brown hair was done up in an elaborate twist, the strapless gown looked elegant on her slim figure. I saw her mom in the front row, beaming in a long maroon lace and chiffon dress, turn toward her daughter as she arrived at the altar. I imagined she saw the same double exposure I had in my mind, this magazine-picture bride in a long tulle veil, and skinny teenage Jeni curled up on the shabby blue dorm basement couch bent over her poetry notebook, writing.

The First Night of Four Years

I remember the car ride in.
Detective Skewes told me I'd be fine.
I remember the fat black lady that did my intake.
She told me to take off my socks.
I remember putting cold shampoo on every crevice
of my body that had hair on it—
felt like a flea bath.
I remember the size-ten underwear
I had to tie in a knot on my hip
cause DCF's so fuckin' cheap.
I remember crying for fifteen minutes
because the bitch said my navel ring
had to come out
but it didn't want to.
Needless to say, it didn't
I remember sliding my skinny arm
into that cage to reach the phone
(I hung up on her anyway).

Jeni

I remember cell #1.
I should, I had it three months.
Then I moved to #4.
I had a mirror.
I remember being flooded with 45 other boys.
Some girls would die for this.
I just wanted to die.
I remember putting my hand up for seconds
'cause food was my only pleasure.
I remember not breathing real air all spring.
Those felonies cost me some good games of football.
I remember the first time I went to the courtyard
separated from population.
The deal was half an hour a day with a supervisor.
I can remember not minding that I was removed from
population—
except that I wasn't the one that needed to be protected.

Jeni and I remain in touch, and have regular lunches with each other. She is living a successful life with a good job, she and Kyle own a home, and she is close to her parents and twin nieces, pictured often with them on Facebook, picking apples or snuggling with them both. I asked her to tell me what creative writing had been for her, and she wrote me these careful words:

> Sharon's creative writing class was better then any class I have ever taken. Even through college no writing class has been able to live up to it yet. Her class was a process. A process that started the first time you met her. A progression that started with an awkward group of individuals, all in a similar situation but with very different needs.
>
> We learned to trust each other as we became better writers. We were taught how to learn about ourselves with simple writing ideas. As our work progressed we would read it aloud to each other. As we perfected our pieces we would read them in front of many. This brought up confidence and whatever that particular poem was about we got some closure from it. By working on something so much you really have to give it thought and that makes you talk about it to perfect it so others will understand.

Along the way we meet people that share the same feelings or situation. These people are part of the process as well. They give you a feeling of understanding and empathy.

So when you ask me if writing was a form of therapy I'd have to say yes. Personally it was probably one of the best forms for me. It also helped me in other therapies I was in at the time. It helped me creatively express myself and brought issues that no one person could find for you. You had to find them in yourself.

Jeni

Hotchkiss

While Tarray, Chimere, and Jeni were still at Touchstone, I ran into Sarah Tames in the local Grand Union. Sarah was an English teacher and director of the drama program at the Hotchkiss School, an independent, elite boarding school for grades 9-12 in Lakeville, the town in which I lived.

I hadn't seen Sarah in a while and as we talked, she became excited when I told her about the poetry group I'd developed at Touchstone, and insisted I bring the girls to read their poems in their Black Box theatre.

I was hesitant, wondering how the two wildly divergent worlds would mix, could mix. Hotchkiss had long been a bastion of the upper class, though like most private schools, it had begun years ago to diversify its student body in both race and ethnicity. It was still mostly a homogeneous and privileged place, though, with impressive numbers of elegant brick buildings set amidst a swath of green lawns, even a nine-hole golf course. The boys wore jackets and ties and the girls, skirts and pants that had to pass the "non-jean-style" test. All participated in extensive sports and other extracurricular programs in addition to a rigorous academic curriculum.

Touchstone, with its small campus of down-at-heel buildings, its inner-city residents almost all with charges of delinquency and on probation, mostly young women of color, seemed its direct opposite in every way except that the kids in both places were teenagers.

What a clash of cultures, But what extraordinary opportunities for each to see into the other's world, an experience that no textbook or didactic class could give...it is worth considering, I thought.

My sons had both graduated from Hotchkiss in the early '80s, attending as day students, and his time there had been a rough ride for Geoff, who was late to mature. He was short and looked younger than his age. He loved and excelled at sports, but his asthma had made participation in them difficult. In an autobiography Geoff wrote for an English class his first year, he wrote about his life there. Here are some fragments:

> *...When I was younger, my asthma was really bad. I used to*

wake up every night wheezing. I had to go into my parents' room and take my pills and sit down on their bed until the wheezing went away. I couldn't lie down because it was hard to breathe. Sometimes I wheezed so badly that Dad had to give me a shot. I'll always remember how much those shots hurt...

...I was good in sports in grammar school. I was on the soccer team, the basketball team and the baseball team. I used to be in the starting line-up of all three teams. I was the star second baseman on the baseball team. I remember when I got my Rawlings baseball glove for my birthday. I cherished it. I broke it in for weeks before I even used it in a game. I stopped playing baseball, basketball and soccer after eighth grade...

...I used to go to Hotchkiss all the time to play with a friend. I hung around campus a lot, and got to know the place pretty well. I dreamed of going to Hotchkiss when I got older. I applied to Hotchkiss when I was in the eighth grade, determined to get in. I worked really hard on my application; I wrote a twenty-one page essay. I got in to Hotchkiss as I had hoped, but the school was not at all what I had expected...

My older son Matthew did okay, considering the social and emotional support the school lacked at that time, as he had an extroverted personality, big brains, and his father's tolerance for difficulties; but for Geoff, small, shy and looking young for his age, the shortage was overwhelming. He had been teased and bullied that first year, and had bravely written weekly papers about it for his English class. They were corrected for punctuation, grammar, and spelling, but had never a comment on them about their courageous and painful subject matter.

We'd implored him to consider changing schools, but he refused, despite his obvious depression. Eventually he found solace in art, and some outlier friends, so the next few years got somewhat better, but not enough. He never found a way to fit in, and after a few years didn't want to, equating fitting in with selling out.

Geoff's experience at Hotchkiss was what made me decide to go for the reading. Maybe it could give other sensitive kids who'd felt like him, pressured, confused, overwhelmed, a place to go with those feelings. He had been such a compassionate, generous-hearted boy. Being exposed to the Touchstone girls' poems would have been deeply affecting for him and others like him, in a school where such experience was not readily available.

Things were different now, too, at Hotchkiss. There was a Human Development program. There were kind, skilled female counselors in addition to the school psychiatrist, and younger teachers who were more knowledgeable and caring about the needs of adolescents.

And it would be another way to honor his life.

* * *

The Black Box theater was packed with adults and kids; almost all the seats were taken. The girls sat behind me in a line on black molded plastic chairs, dressed in their snug jeans, tank tops and hoodies.

I swept my eyes around the darkened theater, packed with Hotchkiss students and their teachers, cleared my throat, wiped away tears, and began to speak.

My name is Sharon Charde. Nearly four years ago I started volunteering at Touchstone, a residential treatment facility for female juvenile offenders in Litchfield. I wanted to give something back to the community of which I was part. I had no idea what was in store for me. My life has been transformed by the young women you see behind me, as well as the many others who have come before them. Each week we write together and share our lives and stories, we learn from each other. They have brought much needed color to my white world. They have taught me about risking, about opening, about freedom and what it means to have it taken away. They have taught me about how young women who have suffered unimaginable damage and pain can not only survive but shine, and inspire others to have the same courage.

I want to have their voices heard in this world, your world of Hotchkiss. Both my sons graduated from here in the early '80s so I have a special feeling for this place, although it is a different place tonight than it was twenty years ago. I don't think there would have been a program like this back then, and

I know how much it would have benefitted my sons and their classmates, given them a glimpse of lives so different from the privileged ones they took so for granted. So it gives me great pleasure to introduce to you these six Touchstone poets. In their true raw words they will show you that we're all the same under our different skins and genders—we all want to love and be accepted, we're all pushing against injustice and crying out when we are hurt. We're all sisters and brothers in this difficult and beautiful world.

The audience was eager and hungry for their words and the girls did not disappoint, with an over-the-top performance. In the talk-back afterwards, one of the Touchstone girls threw out a challenge to the audience. "What do you think of us?"

An intense dialogue ensued. Teachers had brought their classes, so both kids and adults were present, and neither group held back.

"We think you're amazing, brave," was one response to the question. They asked about what Touchstone was like, but in such a respectful way. It was clear that they were being offered an entirely new world's experience, and they were drinking it in.

My girls were emboldened by all the interest in their poems and their lives and responded in their usual authentic and engaging style, offering the audience the realities of their neighborhoods and daily lives. I commented in my wrap-up that we were all the same, equals really, rowing in a boat together toward being more fully human.

The girls, feeling like stars, left the theater with the staff who'd brought them. Nancy Gaynor, head of Human Development (HD) came up to me and said, "We need you. We have to keep this relationship going."

"We need you too, Nancy. How can we make that happen?" I was amped up by the success of the evening, and together we determined to find a way.

So we planned a meeting for the next month, with dinner at the boathouse by the lake. The administration at Touchstone agreed and was able to send staff members and several of the girls who had performed at the Black Box. Nancy identified a group of interested Hotchkiss girls, many of whom were of color, and they were gracious and kind.

Hotchkiss

But the evening was somewhat awkward—there were too many tables in too small a space and the room felt congested—not the best set-up for comfort with the newness of our experiment, but it was a meaningful first step.

After dinner, I read Sylvia Plath's poem *Mirror* as a prompt.

"I am not cruel, only truthful," says the mirror in Plath's poem. It masterfully explores the tensions between Plath's inner and outer selves, and both groups of girls willingly stripped off their masks in ardent and intense response.

As they left, all were talking animatedly and planning for the next get-together.

Nancy and I sat in the cool May evening by the lake, recounting the night and how to capitalize on its momentum and excitement. We were sure it would have tremendous social value for the students involved.

Eventually we settled on a paradigm that worked—pizza and Oreos in an English classroom and two or three writing prompts, for as many Monday nights as we could carve out of the busy Hotchkiss schedule. There was usually a group of at least ten Hotchkiss girls, and a varying number of Touchstone girls and staff. Touchstone was frequently late; it was a forty-five minute trip through lots of winding back roads, and the various staff members who were assigned to come often got lost or left late due to poor planning or crises that had come up that afternoon.

But because we all were determined to make this unique interconnection work, we pushed the obstacles aside and persisted.

Dennis

Dennis Watlington, who had been one of the first black students at Hotchkiss in 1969, had given a recent reading at the school. I'd bought his book, *Chasing America*, and ripped through it, compelled by his story.

> *I live in two Americas; the White one we sell versus the one that includes us all. The latter is the America I am constantly chasing. As long as I can pay the exorbitant Black tax, a tariff placed upon my admission to the mainstream, I can hold my own in the struggle to juggle both worlds.[4]*

I knew right away I had to ask this man to come and speak to the Touchstone-Hotchkiss group. I was sure he'd be a perfect guest for us, having been a drug addict, in juvenile detention hall, in a biracial marriage, dealt openly with racial issues. He'd had troubles with his parents, gone to prep school, been thrown out of prep school, and been in an honest struggle to see his worlds, both black and white, optimistically. When I called, he said he would be delighted to come, and arrived as promised.

Only three Touchstone girls showed up, and they were an hour late. I was seething, hotter than the waiting pizzas. Dennis had regaled us with stories during the interlude; the girls were rapt, but my anger had distracted me. I'd emailed the recreation director the day before, and spoken to her that day on the phone. "Oh yes," she'd promised, "they'll be there at 5:15."

At times like this, several years into my time at Touchstone, I continued to be forced to lower my expectations further than they already were. *Everything is impermanent, accept things as they are,* I told myself. But I couldn't. Having the hope that things would go smoothly was a trap I could see in theory, but not in practice.

Dennis was a large man, commanding, charismatic. Dressed in a skullcap, olive green t-shirt and black sweats, he told us he'd only been off heroin four months when he'd arrived on campus in 1969 in the president of the Board of Directors' Porsche, replete with bags of clothes just purchased

---

4   Pg. 5, *Chasing America*

from a men's store in Canaan, a nearby town. How ill-prepared he was to deal with the experience that would soon unfold.

When my girls had finally arrived, I handed him the copy of his book I'd brought. "Dennis, will you read something for us?" I asked.

He first picked the part about being sent away as a child to live down south with his grandmother. Then he read a section about race and breaking taboos. I jotted down ideas for prompts from his readings—"How do you walk the tightrope between the races?" "A time you broke a taboo." "What are your thoughts about race? "A time you were sent away."

"Sharon, what's a taboo?" Marissa, one of the Touchstone girls, asked.

"Taboo," I said. "It's something forbidden, something that is not supposed to be spoken about, ever."

Everyone began writing—fast, as it was late and we all knew it. Marissa wrote about her grandmother's taboo on dating a non-Italian.

> *...you see, my grandmother believes that no one*
> *should date or marry a different race*
> *no matter that I, and the rest of my family,*
> *tell her it's 2006 and there are a lot more serious issues*
> *to worry about than that...*

She was the first to read, and then we went around the circle. A black staff member from Touchstone, who'd been a minister in Africa, wrote of his initial belief that AIDS victims were sinners, and how he'd had to revise that belief with a humility gained from regret for his mistakes.

Many of the girls wrote about being sent away, and Athena, one of the teachers who supported our sessions, wrote an intense piece about race, about walking the tightrope, her desire to be black, her guilt at being white, crying as she read. Lacey, one of the blonde and blue-eyed Hotchkiss students, told of shame over her ancestors owning slaves.

> *Of my thoughts about race, I wish it didn't exist. When I was*
> *little I couldn't grasp racism, a black woman was my second*
> *mother. My first crush was on her son. But that was in DC,*
> *the neutral part of the world. It wasn't until I moved to the rare*
> *corner of this country (Texas) where confederate flags stick to*

I Am Not a Juvenile Delinquent

cars and more people speak Spanish than English, that racism came into focus. The stigma is ever-present. My mother, who I think feels more at home in the race that raised her, that "village" which was more kind and loyal to her at times than her own blood, was worried that my bi-racial school (only) included one African-American girl in my grade. I was confused, to say the least. The real thing is that it hurts me. Reading the beginning of "Invisible Man" today I had tears of guilt in my eyes, guilt for being, well, so white. It's distanced me from so many people. I want that boundary gone.

The girls rushed to Dennis as the evening broke up, asking for autographs. No one wanted to leave. I asked him to sign my copy of his book. He took out a Sharpie and wrote:

To Sharon:

The concept of bringing different backgrounds into the same room to share the writing experience is a larger contribution to the craft than most authors make. I'm behind your effort in spirit, and in substance, use me as you see fit.

Love,
Dennis

My head was full of the night's powerful connections, my body felt elastic, almost fluid. All that I'd worked so hard for seemed suddenly possible, bringing all these worlds together in the same space, helping them to communicate with ease and honesty. Dennis and I shared an enormous hug in the foyer before we parted. I had to really stretch to get my arms around him, he was so much bigger and taller than me.

"Sharon, if this was years ago, I'd be standing here looking at my feet instead of looking you in the eye. And we certainly wouldn't be hugging each other. This was great, revolutionary. I can't wait to come back."

We walked out to our cars with the arms of possibility wrapped around our shoulders.

I Should Have Been Happy

Sometime after the three years I'd been at Touchstone, the idea of putting the girls' poems into a book began to grow. I'd never done anything like this before, but I was sure I could figure out a way.

Thanks to a friend's connection, the Brookfield Playhouse had offered to do a February 14 performance of Eve Ensler's *The Vagina Monologues* and donate the proceeds to Touchstone. This compelling play was performed all over the world on Valentine's Day each year to highlight awareness of domestic violence and raise money to combat it; we certainly qualified as a recipient.

And Eve had put out a call for kids to write poems on the topic, "What The World Would Look Like Without Violence." *What an absolutely perfect prompt,* I'd thought.

But even better, the Playhouse had invited them to come on stage to read those poems after the performance. Michelle Sarofin, the then-director and her supervisor, cooperated fully with the whole project, getting the necessary parental permissions for the girls to read the play and be present for it. They even planned a bake sale and had the girls make jewelry to sell before the performance, and made sure the girls had the clothes the director had requested.

My adrenaline was running high.

It would be the perfect opportunity to have the chapbook of the girls' poems I'd envisioned published and sold. All I had to do was figure out how to produce it.

To begin, I needed money. I got it, from a grant I applied for, and a generous contribution from a local women's group.

I needed permissions galore from all the girls, their parents, parole officers, and guardians. I got those too, with Michelle's supportive help.

Now I needed poems. I had plenty of those, but how to choose? I did the same thing I'd done for my own collections—spread piles of typed copies of their poems all over the floor of my study and just stared at them for a while, then began moving them without thinking too much into an "arc" that felt like a punch to the gut—*I'm Dying Inside, Do You Know My Pain?*, *Mother, Where Are You?*, and many more that answered my passion to have their voices heard in the world.

On fire in the introduction, I wrote how the girls had transformed their short lives into art, and of how their poems both could open our hearts and help us to understand why they were "locked up" in a way scholarly articles and studies never could.

I Am Not A Juvenile Delinquent would be the perfect title. It faultlessly captured my passion to have the world see that these extraordinary young women were so much more than the label society had placed on them.

A friend recommended a talented designer. She did a simple cover, in red, white, and black, with "Not" in italics so that it stood out, as it needed to, from the other words. She found a publisher in Torrington who would print the books.

The day before the play, I drove an hour each way, skidding and sliding in my black Saab, to the small garage printing press in a snowstorm to pick them up.

In the frenzy of production, I'd never really thought about possible sales. I had just known I *had* to do this, and like everything else I'd pulled off at Touchstone, I just did it.

We sold dozens of copies to the big crowd that night. One man even paid fifty dollars for one! Everyone who bought a book wanted the autographs of the girls, who danced around after the show loudly and jubilantly, signing books and accepting congratulations and hugs from men in suits and women in fur coats.

Dressed in white blouses and black skirts and pants, they had done an awesome job of reading their "What The World Would Look Like Without Violence" poems at the end of the play—the director had come to Touchstone several times to give them professional rehearsals which had resulted in a terrific performance.

It had been shocking to me that almost none of the girls could imagine such a world, believing it would be a dull place. Most of them thought the elimination of violence was impossible.

In a surprise ending to their reading, the girls had made a public presentation of a gift and a poem they'd written for me:

How can we thank you for all that you've done?
Look at how far all of us have come—
You helped us overlook our past and prepare for the future.
We all love you.

All of us—audience, actors, staff, and girls—went out soaring into the snowy dark.

* * *

In 2004, I decided to bring out a full-length, perfect-bound collection (a chapbook, after "chapter," is an abbreviated version). It would also be called *I Am Not A Juvenile Delinquent*, and I would use the same designer and the same process. I found a bigger, more professional publisher in Michigan.

We had the money now, from what we'd raised the night of the play, and a large contribution from a line item in Touchstone's budget. After the great success of *The Vagina Monologues*, the program and I had new stature.

We were hot. And I was riding high. The girls had been so inspired and elated to see their poems in print. I knew that a bigger collection would bring even more positive feedback. It was all what I'd dreamed of, at last.

Wasn't it?

I had a thousand books printed, and debuted *I Am Not A Juvenile Delinquent* at the first annual poetry festival I planned for the summer of 2004. *Why not?* I thought. I invited all my women poet friends to come and read with the girls; I created a contest for the girls, with prizes for the best poems and judges to choose them.

The evening was preceded by the usual chaos and challenge—but at least the girls who had behavior problems could still participate, as there was no going off-grounds involved. The weather was perfect and lots of people came. I'd asked my poet friends to bring work of theirs that resonated with that of the girls, and they did not disappoint. It was another wonderful mingling of worlds, and because poetry is so joining, it worked. The festival got bigger and better each summer, until I ended my work there in 2009.

I submitted the book to the National Council On Juvenile Delinquency's PASS (Prevention For A Safer Society) Awards competition, and it won an award.

* * *

I should have been happy about all this. And I was, sort of. The writing project I'd begun five years before in the dreary dorm basement with those seven girls was now officially a flagship program at Touchstone, acknowledged by most there as a powerful adjunct to treatment. Preoccupied with planning all the special events and readings, hosting an evening monthly poet/performer, running the new Advisory Board, typing all the poems, driving down to Litchfield, sometimes several times a week, and meeting with the Hotchkiss group, I was working harder than ever. Too swamped to think about anything other than Touchstone, I was farther from the impossible truth of my loss.

But under the overdoing, or conceivably because of it, my grief still nested in deep, my brokenness a daily rupture. It felt so heavy and hard to wake up each morning and face the work of living. John and I spent some of these years in marital therapy to sort out the mountains of mistakes and disappointments that Geoff's death had blown into powerful relief. Hungry demons grabbed me in the deep silence of the mindfulness retreats I made twice a year, pushing the emptiness I felt into my face.

I'm not sure I knew my work at Touchstone was a constant race from my sorrow. I didn't know that that sorrow would never leave me, and anyway, part of me didn't want it to. It was alive, real, a needed connection to Geoff. It belonged to me as nothing else had. But my life had been split into before and after by my child's death, and I was compelled to make the after part meaningful, I did know that. My love for the girls and all that it took to keep close to them relieved me, filled that greedy emptiness much of the time. So I soldiered on at Touchstone, despite its paradoxical burdens of success and defeat, my exhaustion and stress.

Looking back, I see that Touchstone had become an escape instead of a destination, though I didn't understand that then.

I needed to turn it into a bridge to something new.

What I Want My Words to Do to You

In the following years, out of the ten I volunteered at Touchstone, we were invited to participate in the Teen Dating Violence Summit at the State Capital, the SAFE-T (Sexual Abuse Free Environment For Teens) Program, a Litchfield High seminar that used *I Am Not A Juvenile Delinquent* for its discussion groups, many school readings, performances in cafes, at a graduate class at Sacred Heart University in Fairfield, and a bioethics class at Yale University. Directors came and went at Touchstone, as did staff and therapists and girls. I continued to put on a poetry festival each summer and Artwell readings in early June, which were attended by many, more each year.

We were invited to read at chapel, the required weekly assembly for the whole student body at Hotchkiss, 570 kids plus faculty, in Elfers Hall, the new concert auditorium that rivaled Seiji Ozawa Hall at Tanglewood in its exquisite beauty.

The chapel talk was supposed to offer inspiration to the students, give them something new to ponder. I felt sure that we could accomplish this. We had all the usual problems in preparation, but my spirited, brave girls came through, with the exception of one who had been caught kissing a girl the night before.

Lacey, the student who'd written about racism when Dennis had come, passionate about her participation in this group, insisted on introducing us, long blonde hair swinging, in tight black pants and a cool jacket. Shanique, a prolific poet in our latest group, threw out the net with her poem *What I Want My Words To Do To You*, and grabbed them all, setting the tone for the rest of the reading.

What I Want My Words to Do to You

when I speak I want you to listen
every sentence every breath every pause
I want this to sink inside of you
I want you to know what type of shit I go through
what kind of life I live the battle I fight from day to day

when I speak I don't want your sympathy or your pity
or your everything's gonna be all right

why cry if this ain't ya life? just listen marinate in what I say
when I speak I want to be visible undressed alive

living in your spirit floating in your bones
I speak the truth the whole truth and nothing but it don't
say a word

hush ya mouth I'm not finished yet hear me out this one
time don't shut me down
I tell you this is visible indelible

don't be in denial
open your mind open your heart open your wings

because this is what I want my words, my verse to do to you
my words are powerful and strong

maybe that's why sometimes I feel so alone
I don't think before I speak I just say what's on my mind

that's freedom of speech right?
If I ain't doin' no crime and you didn't like what I just spit out
don't blame me if you can't take the truth

it may hurt a lot but trust me it will be better for you
my words are my protectors my shield for life

without my words I'd probably go outta my mind
my words make me feel whole

my words are like glitter and gold
my words to you may be nothing but lip

> but the words I state the words I form into a sentence
> that says something of value to me
>
> my words
> my words
> my words

The huge hall was completely silent when they finished. The Hotchkiss girls said even the football players had been transfixed.

Movie Stars

Jon Baskin came up from New York with a cameraman and a sound woman on a sunny summer day in 2006. He didn't have enough money to film us for more than that one day and the Artwell performance that was soon to follow, but his intent was to make a short film that could be used to pitch to various possible producers for a longer one. He was not to be successful in that attempt, but created a poignant portrayal of our poetry group process and its culmination in the Torrington reading. The girls were articulate in their interviews with him, and I was able to get much across in mine about my aspirations for them and their poems.

Everyone was excited about the cameras on campus. They followed the girls in their rooms, eating breakfast, then us in the dorm basement, gathered together on the couches with our notebooks and pens, the typed pages I'd returned from the week before. It had become my practice to bring in cakes and gifts for girls who were celebrating birthdays. That day happened to be someone's birthday, so there was a party atmosphere, lots of singing and blowing out candles, big wedges of my chocolate cake before we wrote.

Rontae, prefacing her poem by speaking of how my group gave everyone permission to say what couldn't be said elsewhere in the program, or even in ordinary life, and how helpful that had been to her and the other girls, opened the film with *My Virginity*.

My Virginity

Damn, I lost it so long ago
I can't even remember the beginning.
All I know is that I was very young—
Hold up!—I remember how it begun...

It was in a closet—a deep toy box on top—
all of a sudden, that's the night
my cherry popped.

I Am Not a Juvenile Delinquent

From then, the fucking never stopped.
I was only a child.
But yet I was so fast and so wild.
I had many guys.
They were in, then out, of my life.
I wanted to be filled up
but I felt so empty.
Just a little girl—
very lonely.

Now here I am, wise and ready—
but this shop is closed for repairs.
She's had too many NO GOOD MEN
who didn't care. There's nothing sacred
any more. It was stripped naked
right down to the core.
If only I could take it back.
Shit—I might as well—all the times
I had sex—man, that shit was work.
Now I'm in here—where did it go?
It is weird because I really don't know.
He lied to me when he said
we would get married.
So I thought it was okay
and lost my virginity.
I can't get it back—it's gone forever.
God said it's my temple—something to treasure…

Now it's too late—
ain't shit I can do.
This isn't how I should have treated it, you.
I lost my virginity and can't find it anywhere.
If I could do it again
I damn sure wouldn't share.

In the film, flipping my blowing hair from my eyes, I spoke about the necessity of reflection, which the writing, listening, and reading encouraged. I talked about the special power of writing in community. But much better than my words, the film showed that process actually happening.

Jon wanted to feature the healing aspect of the work for both me and the girls. I was uncomfortable with that. Healing for anyone had not been my goal in coming to Touchstone, despite the fact that it often seemed to be occurring. He kept pushing, though, finally successful in getting me to bring in pictures of Geoff. In the film, I was shown sitting on a bench by the pond, pulling the pictures from a canvas bag and briefly displaying them as I answered his questions about how my son had died.

He really captured my sorrow in that shot.

"Healing happens when you're doing work you love," I said, surprising myself.

Part 3

Turning Point

"A wild patience has taken me this far."
—Adrienne Rich

Miranda

Despite new buttressing and smoother operations during my last few years at Touchstone, the genre of girls was changing. There was more abusive behavior on campus; staff members were sometimes assaulted. I heard reports of things like chairs and bottles being thrown, and the cops were called more frequently. The girls with a violent history had formerly been sent to Steppingstone, but we seemed to be getting more of them.

At some point, Touchstone had been dedicated as a facility for girls who had been traumatized sexually and physically, but the mix had become unbalanced. It didn't seem the program was a safe container anymore, for them, or anyone.

Or maybe Connecticut's cities and neighborhoods were just producing kids who were more pugnacious. Donna, another staff support, and I talked about that.

"Donna, don't you think the girls are different now than they used to be?" (I was thinking of Jeni, Chimere, and Tarray's "generation" of residents.)

"Yes, Sharon, they are. Absolutely."

I had the same discussion with Denise, the longtime school secretary.

"Denise, there are so many violent girls here, so much more acting out, it seems. Is it different now, do you think, than it was when I first came, when you first came?"

"It is different," she said thoughtfully. "There have been so many generations of girls having babies, growing up to repeat the same lives they've had, without breaks in the cycle, that they're getting steadily worse."

I pushed on. The shabby old dorm had been torn down and a capacious modern one built in its place. There were more girls to reach.

Especially Miranda and Molly.

The Monday after Easter, in my eighth year there, I met with the three girls who weren't on school vacation, bringing in chocolate rabbits for everyone. Two of them eagerly unwrapped theirs and gobbled them down. Miranda pushed hers aside. "I don't like this kind," she said, shoving her bunny to the other girls. She was angry, snappy, didn't like any of my prompts.

I read a poem from a book of work by women prisoners that I thought would be a perfect prompt—*We Would Like You To Know.*

"I don't like that one, Sharon."

"How about this one? It's called *I Love You To Death.*" It was an intense poem about an abusive relationship. The other girls and Donna began to write right away.

"I don't like that one either, Sharon." She was as sullen and whiny as a toddler.

I tried three more times. "No, Sharon, I can't write about any of those."

We were meeting in the "media room" in the new dorm, so called I guess because it contained one old computer and a desk. The girls had pulled the side tables in front of the couch so they could write more easily.

But Miranda refused to open her notebook. Last week at Hotchkiss, though, she'd been animated and eager to write, had written two terrific poems to my prompts.

My friend Elizabeth Thomas had written a poem called *Lies My Mother Told Me,* which had just been read on NPR. When I heard it, I'd thought it would make a prompt the girls could really relate to. It was, finally, for Miranda.

Lies My Mother Told Me

I can really only remember
the two times my mother lied to me—

I must have been seven or eight
I remember this so clearly—
I was watching Bambi—
the part where the mother deer dies—
I started crying and ran to mom

mom, she died!
who? she asked
the momma deer
it's okay, I'm here
but you won't be here—not forever—
what if you die?
(it was like a foreshadowing of the future)

Miranda, I'll always be here
I promise

then a couple of years later she died unexpectedly
a heart attack—
why would she make a promise
she knew she couldn't keep?
you know you're not supposed to break promises

then she promised to take me to Disney World
she never got a chance—

Miranda had come into the group sometime in my seventh year there; she'd wanted to join for months and a space in our popular sessions had finally become available. From the beginning, she'd been truly committed to writing, maybe in some way more than any of the others except Molly—and of course, Ellie, Chimere, Tarray and Jeni from way back.

I loved that about her.

Miranda's huge pain informed her writing, but also kept her from it. There were weeks she'd gone AWOL, was on a tight, in the hospital, or just too depressed to come. Sometimes she'd come and write for a while and it would be too much for her and she'd ask to leave.

Always, Miranda was on the edge, the slender lip between living and wanting to die. She was a truly beautiful girl, shapely and slim, with a bit of Native American look to her (she said she was an eighth Native American). Her hair was jet black; she had worn it long, short, pulled back in a ponytail, and everything in between. It was prettiest to me when it was framing her delicate face, with big hoop earrings peeking out.

Because her guardian "father" had been a manager at Kohl's, the department store, she had a large wardrobe of attractive clothes, sundresses, pants and feminine blouses, and dressed up more than the other girls. But when I first met Miranda, she often wore huge sweatshirts and long-sleeved tees—she was starving herself then, and cutting up her arms with razors almost daily.

She was obsessed with death—her mother's and her own.

One day my prompt was a poem that was a question-and-answer dialogue between a living person and his dead relative. She immediately set pen to paper and wrote.

Mother-Daughter Dialogue

mom
no answer
mom?
no answer
mom can you hear me when I talk to you?
no answer
mom!! I scream
no answer
are you watching me? do you see me? can you hear me?
no answer
why don't you ever respond? ever since I was nine you
haven't responded—
no answer
do you know that for once I made the honor roll?
no answer
mom, I'm getting lonely, scared and depressed—can't you
show me, can't you answer me?
no answer
where are you?
no answer
mom, if you can hear me, why did you die?
still no answer

When I got home I wrote her a note:

> Miranda,
>
> I've been thinking about your last poem about your mom.
> I wanted to tell you something I've done that has helped
> me in dealing with my son's death and my strong desire to
> communicate with him.
> First of all, here is my mantra: "Pick something to believe and
> believe in it like God."
> Since we have no idea what happened to those we love (no one
> has come back to tell us) we can decide what to believe. You can
> decide that your mother can hear you and believe that. Ask her
> for a sign. And wait carefully, patiently, until something happens
> that day of asking that feels like an answer (seeing a butterfly, a
> generous thing someone does for you, a big and unexpected hug,
> a dream about her, some kind of gift). I do this (but not too much
> or it loses its magic, and you pester the dead loved one!) when
> I really need to hear from Geoff—like on Mother's Day or my
> birthday or a holiday.
> Also I used to find it helpful to go to his grave and talk to him. I
> don't need to do that so much anymore. I would write him letters
> telling him about the family and what we were doing and read
> them to him. I felt sure he could hear me.
> I hope this helps.

She never mentioned the letter, so one day I asked her about it.

"Did you ever get the note I sent, Miranda?"

"Yes."

"Did it help at all?"

"No, Sharon," she said. "Not really."

She was in a love affair with drugs, as well as with cutting. I had thought
she was okay for a while, but her poems were telling a different story.

Miranda

Feeling Good

it's the rush
to my head
to my brain
to my body
my eyes

it's the feeling I get
after I've just smoked some weed
or snorted some pills

it's also the feeling I get
right after I tear my wrists away

it's the feeling in the moment
that I'm getting high
the feeling of just being bad
of being told not to do it
but then doing it anyway
and feeling the power
feeling like I'm in control

it's the feeling I get when I'm actually high
feeling like I have no problems
feeling great inside
being distracted
not worrying about the past—
today or tomorrow—

when I cut—
yeah, it hurts
but it feels good
you think I'm crazy
that I'm different
but no—
I'm one of many

the feeling I get

I Am Not a Juvenile Delinquent

when I cut, scratch, pick or rub
it makes me feel like I'm in charge
no one else
no one can stop me

no one but me
the blood
the red

it's an infatuation
it attracts the eyes
it wants to see more and more

so here I am introducing you to it
it's my friend—
it's my adrenaline

Miranda was one of the very few Touchstone girls who had ever given me a gift.

At one of our sessions, she handed me a glass plate to which lace had been affixed, I guessed, with heat and glue. There were two roses and ferns beneath them on each end of the plate—they looked real, pressed. A mahogany plate stand came with it.

"I made this for you this weekend, Sharon. Be careful with it."

"So beautiful," I said, moved and surprised by her kindness. "I will find a perfect place for it in my home." Miranda told me how she and her grandma had created it together in the kitchen, and a rare smile lit her face.

"I will always think of you when I see it," I said, tears stinging my surprised eyes.

Miranda

The Boston Trip

It seemed like everything at Touchstone was always waiting for the beginning of something else. Often in a defeatist mode, I mostly expected the something-elses to be negative. But one day, after eight years there, an email popped up from a woman who'd been head of the Connecticut Girl Scouts, and in that role, had come to one of our annual poetry festivals as well as the Teen Dating Violence Seminar. She was now the director of an organization in Cambridge called The Center For New Words, whose mission was to get women's voices heard in the world. She wondered if they could sponsor the girls to come and read in Boston; the Center would cover all expenses.

I decided right then I'd do whatever it took to make it happen.

At our meeting two weeks before the Boston trip, I'd planned to create the group "I Am Not A Juvenile Delinquent" poem in preparation for our Boston performance, hoping it would energize and excite the girls for the trip and help them to stay on their levels, but first I had to talk about the release forms that needed signatures, as we would be filmed by WGBH, Boston public television.

"You're all going to be on TV," I said. "TV that people all over Boston watch, not just a community channel. But this means we'll have to clean up the language in your poems—no 'fucks' or 'shits'—that kind of language is not allowed on television. But you *have* to get these release forms signed."

Molly, one of our best poets, had just been on two overnights out of state, so her parole officer hopefully would be on board for permission. Molly was doing so well now. When she'd first come to Touchstone, she had been thin and pale from her long addiction to drugs, and uninterested in participating in much of anything.

In many ways Molly was atypical for Touchstone. Her mother ran a Montessori school, her hair was long and blonde, her drug abuse was flagrant. Like Jeni and Chimere, it had taken her a while before she'd decided to join the poetry group. When she had, she'd quickly warmed to it and become very committed. Bright and gifted, she used the time to transform her collection of terrifying and dangerous drug escapades, family issues, and a multiplicity of friends' deaths into skillfully written poems.

She and Miranda were particularly bonded to each other. They came from the same town in Connecticut, both were in love with drugs, and both loved to write. They would remain friends for years.

Molly was anxious about being in Boston again, possibly seeing old dealers, as she'd spent four months living on the street there as an addict. The consequence of a possible choice to run and do drugs again was ten years in prison (a condition of her probation).

Though I'd hoped that would be a sufficient deterrent, I was worried too. I'd learned from Molly, more than any of the drug-using clients and friends I'd known, how powerful was the siren call of drugs. And Touchstone was not a drug rehab program; I thought that's what she really needed. I asked her once if anyone from here took her to NA (Narcotics Anonymous) meetings.

She laughed.

"They're a big waste of time, Sharon. The last one I went to, I got four new dealers. No one wants to be at those meetings—they all have to be there because of court."

"Good point," I said.

Before we wrote the group poem, I asked them to read the typed poems I'd handed back. Miranda wanted to go first, with the one she had written when she'd been recently hospitalized.

Girl, Listen

you've heard of it
I've tried it
I've been there
I've done that

girl, listen

there's nothing you can say or do
that will make me judge you
not care for you
or even forget you

I've gotten high on weed
and moved on to worse drugs like meth
I've had sex
believe me I'm no angel—

and when the pregnancy tests came in
I cried because of the results

I've been raped before
I've been called a slut
I've been called a whore
I've been arrested for assault

yeah, that's right
I got high and pulled out a knife

I lost my mom
at the age of nine

and then two weeks later
my grandpa died

I used to lie
I used to steal
I've run away
I've been restrained
(that was just yesterday)

and not too long ago
I hung and tried to kill myself

so what I'm going to do
and I hope you do too

is don't give up

I Am Not a Juvenile Delinquent

because there's a lot in life we need to achieve

life will get better
we just have to believe

We just have to believe, I thought to myself, *we just have to believe.*

I explained to them how we would create this poem, as we had in each session over the years. I said each girl should call out a line as it came to her and I would assemble everyone's lines into a complete piece.

I read another *I Am Not A Juvenile Delinquent* poem for inspiration. The girls got off to a slow start, but quickly picked up speed.

"I am happy turned to sad," Miranda said.

"I'm the whisper that keeps you screaming," Molly said.

"I'm the drug that keeps you fiending," another added.

But they soon tired of this and wanted to write their own *I Am* poems. Molly had to leave for a family session at 4:30, so we lost her strong voice. This particular breakdown had never happened before; usually the girls loved to do the group poem and got really into the experience. I decided to go with their wishes, though, thinking I could just lift the lines we needed to fill the poem out from their individual poems.

And that's what I did.

I Am Not a Juvenile Delinquent

I am going to tell you the raw truth
I am going to ask are you ready well here it is
I am happy turned to sad
a whisper that keeps you screaming
a drug that keeps you fiending
I'm the person you pushed aside
I'm a girl who wants to die
I'm a dream turned to nightmare
the sidewalk you spit upon
the cracks you walk over

I'm a fire that's uncontrolled
the gun you want to hold
the story left untold
some call me nice
others call me bold
I'm the greatest of all achievements
but a person with a head full of air
I'm the girl next door
I'm a junkie
I'm a soldier ready for war
I'm the person on the corner making money
I put food in my family's mouth to eat
I'm not going to tell you what you want to hear
I'm smart and pretty
nobody you need to pity
I am not who you think I am
I'm a wisher, a believer
I like to fantasize
I am a faker
a pretender
a young girl who hasn't gotten anywhere yet
a pair of jeans that just doesn't fit
my mother's on drugs
I am me but maybe her
where are you, daddy?
I'm the person who makes you forget what you enjoyed
but remember what you survived
just look into my eyes
tell me what you see
do not label me
I am............(say names)
I am NOT a juvenile delinquent

I Am Not a Juvenile Delinquent

Getting There

Donna joined us for the meeting before Boston; she was our regular support staff now. I liked Donna a lot. She was rock-solid dependable, older than most of the other staff, adored the girls but didn't put up with their sometimes entitled behavior. Having three kids to whom she was clearly a loving and firm parent made generational boundaries and executive functioning come easily to her, unlike to some of the younger staff.

She was also very funny. A sense of humor went a long way when one worked at Touchstone.

"Get me some water, Donna," Miranda called out.

"I'm not your slave," says Donna. "Any reason you can't get it?"

Artrese, a statuesque African-American young woman who often wore colorful head wraps, melted into the couch. She said little, especially now, after her painful recent breakup with another resident. Hard to know what she was thinking. I fretted that she would decide to drop out at the last minute.

We had a perfect rehearsal. I could hardly believe it. Ja'Keria was fine with reading poems written by other girls in addition to a few short ones of her own. Artrese hesitated over *When I Was Five Years Old*— a hard poem to read—but all supported her and she read it well.

"What if I cry when I read it?" she said.

"It'll be okay," I said. "Just cry and keep reading. People will understand."

Everyone performed their poems well, and they did the *I Am Not A Juvenile Delinquent* poem without a hitch. They even looked up at the ends of their poems.

"Girls, you are beautifully prepared for this exciting trip. I am so proud of you. I wish Donna could come with us, but it's her daughter's birthday. Jess, Kaneisha, and Lindsay will be great, though, and I know we'll have a fantastic time."

At that moment, anyway, I was sure of it.

• • •

The day we were to leave for Boston, I arrived at Touchstone at 9:00 a.m. Ja'Keria helped me unload my bag and the box of books. Jess was busy with last-minute details—trying to find gas cards for the vans, and getting the girls' meds—so we actually didn't leave until about 10:00.

We were due at Lesley University for a tour at 2:00, and despite the struggle with Boston traffic, we made it, only to find out that the plans relayed to us had been totally changed. I berated the flustered young man who'd met us in place of the promised group of young women with whom we were to have shared lunch.

Everyone was quiet, listening to me. I was the one who'd pushed for the trip, and so soon it was going awry. Unnerved and frustrated at this glitch, my body coiled, my hands made fists. I began to sweat. I'd expected things to go smoothly here, a relief from Touchstone's dysfunction.

Once again, I was heavily invested in outcomes, in success, forgetting my Buddhist aspirations. I wanted the girls to feel special and happy, to feel that coming all this way was worth it. And, if I admitted it, I wanted to feel validated and rewarded for my effort, get the gold star.

Instead of being enthusiastic, the girls were non-committal, even a little bored, I thought. But maybe, as they'd told me before, it was all just a cover for the emotions they didn't want to show. Maybe they were anxious, uneasy, out of their safe and familiar environment.

I couldn't know, didn't know.

But I was absolutely certain of this: I didn't want to be the only one excited about this trip.

The guy, slightly chastened, hustled somewhere to recheck plans, and soon we were joined by a gracious woman from Admissions who sat with us while we ate our chicken Parmesan sandwiches. After lunch, we walked over to the green Victorian admissions building with her, and settled into soft velvet armchairs around a fireplace while she told us more about the school and the admissions process.

Dominique had boasted on the way over that she wanted to attend Harvard, as that's where Obama had gone. She wanted to become a lawyer, she said. She could, with her forceful voice, I suppose, given a huge amount of supportive education and full-time mentoring. Miranda wanted to go to college, absolutely, she declared, in art and photography. And in a few weeks she would become a ward of DCF, so, if she could stay stable, graduate from high school, and qualify for college, they would pay tuition. Artrese—who had recently been introduced to dance by our school principal, who had taken her to New York to see a performance—proclaimed she would go to Juilliard for ballet and that was that. Ja'Keria showed no interest in our discussion and Molly didn't say much, but of all the girls, she had the best chance, I thought.

She had some understanding of what college would actually mean—studying hard, dealing with a lot of frustration, maintaining an independent life in the face of no structure and many temptations. She had insight, excellent grades, and realistic goals.

As we walked along Mass Ave., Molly was agitated, constantly scanning the streets. I tried to distract her with conversation about her future plans. She'd told me that she was going to move to Washington, DC after she graduated from high school. She'd live with a friend and try to get into college, "anywhere that will take me." She'd determined that the move would come after probation was over, take her away from her friends in the Connecticut drug world.

I told her about my alma mater, Trinity College in Washington, DC. She seemed interested. I grabbed at the bait, offering to call as soon as I got home and do anything I could to help her get in. She'd be taking the SATs the following Saturday, and was actually studying for them now with the help of a Touchstone teacher. I thought she'd be a perfect bet for Trinity, which now reached out to large numbers of DC city kids with Pell grants and lots of support.

Maybe the seeds sown this afternoon mostly hit dry ground, I thought, *but maybe some could sprout in the future.* I'd wanted to show them a world outside their comfort zone. That was the teacher in me, again.

And the woman with stupid hope.

Cloud Place

It was a relief to be alone in my room for an hour. I lay down on the motel-generic flowered bedspread for a few minutes before taking off my jeans and getting dressed for the evening. The bed was hard, too hard for my bad back, but I'd deal with that later. My son Matthew and his wife were on their way to Cloud Place, as well as my ever-supportive husband. Matthew and Hedi had never seen the girls perform, though they had been privy to many hours of conversation about their exploits, poems, and the ups and downs of Touchstone life.

Tonight, at last, they could see for themselves how terrific and talented the girls were.

I pulled a short gray wool dress over black tights and wrapped a long orange scarf around my neck. After adding black cowboy boots and big silver hoop earrings, I was ready to go. When I went out to the hall, I saw that the girls had all made an effort for the evening and looked awesome. Molly wore a tiny black and white dress with tights and high black boots, Miranda had on a black bustier with a white shirt and black pants. Artrese wore a low-cut black tank top and one of her colorful headwraps.

It was a soft fall evening. The streets were lively, and the venue was in a great neighborhood. I was concerned, as usual, about audience—this was an election debate night. John McCain and Barack Obama would have their final exchange of the season, and I was sure it would keep people from coming. As we climbed the three flights of stairs to the Cloud Place auditorium, I fretted about potential crowd size.

The three women with whom I'd been corresponding for months about plans for this trip were all there in the dark black and brick room, setting up chairs and a table with information about The Center For New Words programs. They put our books out too, and the girls went to the mike to practice while I considered how to best position them.

They did a perfect job of figuring out how to do the group poem, *I Am Not a Juvenile Delinquent*, passing the mike from person to person.

A few people arrived, and then my family came in. There were hugs all around, and I introduced Matthew and Hedi to each girl, filled with a surprising gust of emotion. Dr. Bakal, executive director and founder of the entire North American Family Institute, arrived with his wife and shook my hand warmly.

I'd invited him, knowing he lived in Brookline, a suburb of Boston, never imagining he would come. It meant a lot to me that he would actually get a chance to see what the program could do for the girls. A dear friend arrived with her partner and his daughter, a Lesley student, and I could see that my invitees were at this point, a third of the audience. Not a big turnout, but enough to begin. More straggled in as we went on, and by the time we got to the talk-back, there was a decent-sized group in the folding chairs, though not the crowd I had hoped for.

My head spun with disappointment and shame.

One of the women from the Center introduced me and I began with lots of thank-yous. The girls sat behind me, and I could feel their excited expectancy like an adrenaline tonic. Beginning to feel better, I gave my introduction:

> It is difficult
> to get the news from poems,
> yet men die miserably every day
> for lack
> of what is found there.
>
> William Carlos Williams forgets women and children in his poem—those were the days of the white male writing most of what we all read—poetry and prose—but he speaks to an important point, especially at this moment in history, when the world as we knew it, or thought we knew it, is in tatters.
>
> We need poems; poems speak the language of the soul. They call from beneath the surface of our lives, exclaim to us the direct experience of truth. Molly and Miranda, Ja'Keira, Dominique, and Artrese call out to us tonight to listen to voices that must be heard in this world and too often are not.
>
> Their poems are filled with cries to be noticed, to be heard, to be seen. Their poems tell us of horrific personal experiences, of wise

reflections, of profound desires. Their language is raw and real, their details will sear your ears and your hearts. You will not go away untouched.

Dominique began. She had a confident voice and powerfully cadenced poems. She read *Statistic Me* first, and I breathed freely for the first time all day. Everything was going to be okay, big audience or not.

Here is an excerpt from her second poem, which she read with a voice that matched the strength of her words:

Little Soldier

pain is something that I hate
something that I feel
you can shut me down
but I can't shut you up
like you have authority
and I'm your little slut
like you and little quick fast
you betta think again
'cause this young girl
doesn't take shit from anybody
been disrespected her whole life
taken advantage of
and you know what you can do?
back off, I'm ready
and I've been in training
for this little thing you people call war
just so you know—
I've brought along confidence, smarts
faith and most of my dignity
it will never be taken

....

the power I have
it comes from within
you thought you beat me
you had to think again

I Am Not a Juvenile Delinquent

because this little soldier told you
you lose and I win

Ja'Keria went next and read a few of her short poems and Kimani's *My Neighborhood*. Her voice had such a melodic quality, both soft and strong.

Miranda began her performance with *It's Gonna Be Amazing*, reading with perfect presence and pitch.

It's Gonna Be Amazing

of course I'll have to die first
dying is the part I'd like to miss
but then what comes after death
who knows
but what I imagine is
golden roads that climb and twist
throughout the marshmallow clouds
the roads go on forever and will never end
angels with white wings and yellow shimmering haloes
that cover their heads
who keep you from falling out of the sky
gates, big gold gates
they aren't locked
so everyone can come in
pets of all sorts—
cats, dogs, hamsters—
anything that was loved
no money because things are free
food, houses—
your favorite everything
there will be rainbows—thousands of them
each one made of all the colors imaginable
there's places where you can go
to check on those you care about who you've left behind
something like a telescope
only there's no glass—
you just look down

Cloud Place

there will be ice cream—
cookie 'n' cream, chocolate, chocolate chip, cookie dough—
all the ice cream you can think of
there's music
rap, R&B, country, classic rock—
all the music you enjoyed
there's no violence—
none at all
it's nothing but a peaceful place
there will be my mom smiling—
she's so happy to be with me again
and there will be my uncle Tom and grandpa
greeting me at the gates
heaven
it's gonna be amazing!

The room hushed as she read her other poems. The girls were looking up at the audience, reading reasonably slowly, and looking attentive and interested. And the audience was holding its collective breath.

Artrese was next, and she took the mike more confidently than I had imagined she would have, opening with her chilling poem, *When I Was Five Years Old.*

When I Was Five Years Old

when I was five years old
I was raped
by a stink-breath drug dealer
just for some pleasure
and to give my mother money
so she could get high
to hide the pain
she was feeling deep inside

she was crying
while I was screaming

she was happy
while I was hurting

she knew it was wrong
'cuz it happened to her
when she was thirteen

but she didn't care about how I felt
she just cared about the drugs
she was about to get

I hit and kicked
punched and spit
but it didn't get him off me

it made it worse
my mother pinned my arms down
while he pushed it inside of me

he huffed and he huffed
and whispered in my ear

I laid there crying
hoping for the pain to go away

when it was done
I cried all day long

kept my mouth closed
and hated him and my mother—
the woman I used to love

I always cried when she read this poem. I had never dreamt that drug abuse could go to such limits, far past all concepts of acceptable behavior.

So the world can bear witness, I thought. *That's why I'm doing this.*

Molly's turn came. She read of her drug abuse and that of her friends, of her love for drugs.

She ended the reading with this poem.

These Are My Friends

this is my friend
the baby that has a baby
(both junkies)
and says I love you in between
pushing opium grains
down its throat

this is my friend
the girl who cuts her arms to ribbons
just to get sewn back together
until she resembles nothing more
than a cruelly made rag doll

this is my friend
the scared little boy who runs
from homeward fists
drinks away his bruises
jumps into a car to party
only to drive neatly
into a splintered tree

this is my friend
the junkie who discovers
he has AIDS
learns the only two he loves
he's passed it on to—
and when the guilt overwhelms
he overdoses on the one thing
that brought him comfort

this is my friend
the child who has no real family
so joins a stand-in
loses everything that is beautiful to him
the day he dies in a war of colors

this is my friend
the girl who never came to school
because she's walked the streets

I Am Not a Juvenile Delinquent

turning tricks
hoping her sister never sees
the things she's seen

this is my friend
the boy who lets his coke rule his life
until the day he takes charge
by silently turning the trigger
against his temple

this is my friend
the murderer who sits in jail
for killing the man
who stole the soul
from his five-year old daughter

lost and scared
my friends huddle in safety
most won't make it to 21
some will never see 18
and for nineteen of them
it's already too late

the rest stay strong
forcing themselves to bear
whatever life throws

these are my friends

The audience rose to its feet, clapping and crying.

The talk-back went on for an hour or more. People wanted to know if writing made them feel better, if writing in a group was helpful, how they had chosen the poems they read tonight, what writing did for them in general. Their answers stunned me. Maybe they really were getting something from the poetry group experience.

Everyone commented on the strength and power of the poems, and the courage it must have taken to read them; many surrounded the girls for more conversation after the evening had officially ended.

The women from the Center took us all out for pizza afterwards and the girls were animated, exhilarated.

Cloud Place

The waitresses brought tall glasses of soda for everyone, steamy deep-dish pizzas in hot black pans, and we all grabbed for pieces, starving after the intense reading and long walk to the restaurant.

The next morning at 8:30, the time we'd agreed to meet, I walked into the motel restaurant. No girls. I told the waiter to expect nine for breakfast and returned upstairs. They'd slept with staff nearby who'd dozed in relays, so no one could have strayed out into the Boston night, but now they were all clumped in one of the rooms—Miranda was sick, she said, and looked tired. Everyone seemed low-energy.

"Okay." I said. "Let's go down and have a nice big breakfast—we all need it. They're waiting for us."

Most everyone ordered eggs, home fries, pancakes, sausage, and cranberry juice. Artrese held out for a bowl of frosted flakes and Jess pretended to be Tony the Tiger, growling and laughing.

Molly told me her mother had chickens, did I want some eggs? She'd bring them in next week.

"That would be great," I said. "Fresh free-range eggs are delicious. I'd love some."

"She lets them roam all over the yard and they eat anything."

"How do the neighbors feel about that? I asked.

"Oh, they're heroin addicts, they don't care." For some reason, this struck me as incredibly comical and I couldn't stop laughing for a whole few minutes.

"Sharon, what's so funny?" They were all laughing with me.

"The neighbors," I said between gasps for breath. "I'm just cracking up."

The day was cloudy but still warm; we took the girls on the Duck Tour, an amphibious vehicle that visited the historic sites in Boston and then lowered itself into the Charles River. I thought it was fun, but they seemed bored. At least it provided a morning history lesson, I thought.

We hurried back down Boylston Street to get into the vans and drive to East Boston High School for the planned afternoon reading.

No one was in a good mood.

The library, where the reading was supposed to take place, was empty.

Finally, a large woman in a voluminous long black and white dress arrived and asked the girls to help her move the tables into a different formation. They acceded, but then plunked down behind the tables and refused to move, insisting they would read from there.

The afternoon continued to unravel. A few students drifted in, and a woman from the Center finally appeared. Jess and I tried to pump up the girls, who slumped in their chairs, apathy radiating around them in sticky haloes. Without a mike, their voices were hard to hear, flat and expressionless. The East Boston girls had good questions and the librarian praised my girls as courageous, but begged them to speak up at their next reading.

Jess told the girls they needed to apologize, that they had behaved poorly. Suddenly, they woke up, all saying "Thank you, thank you," signing copies of *I Am Not A Juvenile Delinquent*, and giving goodbye hugs.

Shame flooded me again, reddening my cheeks, clamping my fists. I took their laconic attitudes personally, deep-sixing the success of last night, drowning in the failure of the afternoon.

I had planned too much. I had trusted too much. I felt guilty and foolish. I blamed myself.

Everyone was drained by the time we got back to Touchstone. I just wanted to go home. I'd done it. They'd done it. Now it was over, and on Monday, we'd be back to regular, ordinary poetry group—no preparing for performances, just writing to prompts again.

I hadn't realized fully how the last few months had held me in their muscular grip. Was it only in the aftermath of these situations that I could wake up and see clearly? I remembered a favorite Buddhist story.

The student asks the teacher, "What is the secret of life?"

The teacher responds, "Wise judgment."

The student asks, "How does one learn wise judgment?"

The teacher answers, "Experience."

The student again queries the teacher, "How does one get experience?"

The teacher replies, "Bad judgment."

Helpless, unforgiving, I watched the innumerable mistakes of my life spin around the dance floor of my tired mind.

Bad judgment? Learning? What was the message I needed to heed?

A part of me reared up, whispered, *Maybe it's time to move on, Sharon.* But I quickly silenced it. There was still too much to do for these girls.

The Rip in Her Jeans

At our next session, I hungrily asked the girls for any feedback about our trip—what had they thought? How had it been for them? Not one of them had a word to say. Donna offered that, when she had come in on Friday afternoon that's all they'd talked about, but I got nothing out of them now.

"When are we going to write?" Miranda was always the one who asked.

"Well, we will, but before we do, you need to produce a thank-you note to the women at The Center For New Words, after all they did for us. They paid for everything, our meals, even our gas."

> *Dear KL, Janet and Ally,*
>
> *We thank you so much—we appreciate all the effort you put forward on our behalf. We enjoyed our short stay in Boston very much—we loved the food, the motel and the duck tour. I, Ja'keria, really appreciated that I was able to have chicken when we went out for pizza.*
>
> *We just want you to know that we are thankful for the opportunity to express ourselves through our poems both at Cloud Place and at East Boston High.*
>
> *We really appreciate all you've done for us.*
>
>

Sincerely,

Dominique, Miranda, Artrese, Ja'keria and Molly
>

"Oh, so you liked the Duck Tour?" I said, surprised.

"I didn't like it when we went in the water," Molly said. "That whole trip brought back too many bad memories of living there...seeing the city." Molly looked glazed today—maybe sad, maybe angry—it was impossible to tell. She had a family session scheduled at 4:30 and would have to leave early. I told her that I had spoken with the Alumnae Office at Trinity about her and there could be a connection. She had actually gone online over the weekend and looked up programs.

"I want to do the School of Professional Studies," she said, "Night and weekend classes."

"That sounds good, Molly."

My mood shifted. That she was actually thinking about college and that perhaps I could help her gain admission made me glad, but then Tarray was always in the back of my mind. I remembered how much more passion about her potential I'd had than she.

"Okay, let's write. First, read your poems from last time and then I'll tell you the prompt."

After they read, I suggested "the first time I..." or "the last time I..." Miranda immediately began to write. She'd been so quiet, and coughing a lot. *Still sick*, I thought.

"Oh I love this poetry writing thing," Dominique, said, and grabbed her notebook. Everything was quiet for a while. Miranda asked to read first.

"Sure," I said "Great, let's hear you."

The Last Time, for Many Things

it was October 12, a Sunday
I can remember what I was wearing—

a hoodie and a pair of jeans with a huge hole
high on my thigh, another low by my knee
and another hole above my knee

my mom left with the twins
to go to a birthday party
while dad and I stayed at home

I was sleeping peacefully on the couch
I had woken up—
dad sat down beside me

we were talking about how I had punched the window
and hurt my hand—he started to rub it—
then removed his hand and lowered it to my knee
he then slid it up towards my body—

I Am Not a Juvenile Delinquent

his hand was now on my thigh
I could feel his cold manly hands rubbing up
the rip in my jeans

next, and I remember this clearly—
(it stays in my head)
he says to me am I making you uncomfortable?
no I say—I was nervous—
I got up to look for the cat
(thinking he might stop)

I grabbed the cat and sat back down
he put his hand back and started to rub—

then he moved his hand to a place he should not have

I felt so scared
fuck that
I was terrified

I got up and said dad I'm going to the party—
he let me go

it's not like this hasn't happened before—
I can remember him taking my hands—and well—
you don't have to know

the thing is it always happened at night
so it was hard to be sure it had really happened

now I'm definite that it happened a lot more
than I was aware of

now my mom's lying about my being home alone with him
I feel betrayed by not just dad but mom—

that was the last time he'll use me as a sex toy—
the last time he'll hurt me

that day was the last time of feeling comfortable around
him—
the last family I'll ever trust
the last people besides my real ones to be called mom and
dad

The Rip in Her Jeans

they're not my family anymore
my dad's mad at me for telling
and my mom's mad too

my life's been ruined

why me
why me
why me

My entire body clenched in fury, disbelief. These were Miranda's *guardians*, her supposed protectors, her mother's best friend and her husband, who took her in after her mother's death.

I suddenly remembered walking next to her in Boston, asking her if she'd been home to see them lately, how it was going.

"Oh, I don't see those people anymore," she said. "As of the 29th, I'm going to be DCF."

I was surprised at the time but didn't say more. Maybe I had asked why, but had gotten no satisfactory answer. Maybe someone had interrupted, or we'd arrived at a destination and the conversation had stopped.

Now I knew why.

"Miranda, that was incredible work," I said, and asked the next reader to start, not wanting to draw unwanted attention to her revelation.

Miranda pulled her navy blue hoodie over her face, and Molly reached out to hold her hand.

"Sweetie, are you crying? Do you need some space?" I asked.

"I want to go back to the house. Take me back to my room."

Donna got up and the two of them left.

I dreamt about Miranda all night long. We were going on a trip. She was in the car with me, and I had put all her stuff inside but then looked for her purse and couldn't find it. She started to cry and said she couldn't afford to buy lunch. I held her close and told her not to worry, that I had money. I found her purse but then lost mine. I saw it lying in the snow next to the car, so went around to the other side to get it, but it was gone. I had been careless with it, and, in the dream, I was now so upset that I couldn't take care of Miranda.

It took me awhile to shake off the dream's residue. It seemed like a warning to me; that if I was not more careful I would lose myself completely in these girls, this place, that perhaps I already had.

Carla

Months ago, it had been determined that I'd need major back surgery to relieve the debilitating pain caused by my spinal stenosis. It was November 7, 2008, the night before the big operation. *Why not gather with the girls at our scheduled Hotchkiss meeting?* I'd thought. *What better place to be?* Otherwise, I'd just be sitting at home, fretful and edgy.

When I walked in, I noticed a CD at my place with a pale yellow cover. Inscribed on it was "Sharon's Get Well CD" in red Sharpie pen.

"Is this from all of you?" I asked, wondering, pleased.

"No," said Carla, sitting next to me, "It's from me. I made it for you."

"What a lovely thing to do," I said, hugging her. "Thank you, sweetie."

Carla was a "fac brat" (meaning her parents were teachers at Hotchkiss and she had lived on campus her whole life). An unusually contemplative young woman, she'd joined the group her first year and had almost never missed a session, except for the semester she spent in Colorado. She had long thick honey-colored hair, like so many of the other pretty Hotchkiss girls, but there was something different about her face. Carla was beautiful, but not in a traditional preppy way. Those penetrating green eyes stayed with you, but could also veil emotion. She held her intensity in a tightly lidded container, rarely letting it seep out. When Carla did eventually cry at her final session, her sobbing was so unstoppable that she got a nosebleed, blood and tears everywhere, embarrassing her mightily.

She'd told me once that the Hotchkiss girls would never take off the masks they had to wear as students there without the Touchstone girls' presence; I knew she was talking about herself. Carla pondered things before she spoke them out loud. She tuned in to people at all levels, and had added a real seriousness of purpose to our group. One night during her first year, in response to the prompt, "Where I come from," she'd written this:

> I come from a place where I've always felt safe, where I've
> always felt confident. I come from playing "secret agent" on the

playground until the sun went down. Where I come from, I know everyone's name.

I go to a place where it's scary to walk down the hallway sometimes, a place where you can't trust everyone you want to. I go to a place where there is no time to play imaginary games, where everything seems all too real. The place where I see a new face every day.

I don't know if the differences between these two places help me or hurt me; there are times when they do both at the same time. Most days I want to go back to where I came from, and forget about the place I go to now. They both have the same address, the same location on a map, yet they are on opposite ends of my life, one the past and one the present. They pull me back and forth until I don't even know where I am anymore.

Molly, Miranda, and Ja'Keria arrived with Donna along with Kimani, a new girl in our group. As soon as I saw Miranda, I realized she was in a bad space again; I could almost see the aura of shadow surrounding her.

I gave "The Last Time I Was In A Hospital" as the first prompt. For the next one, I'd brought in my postcard collection. I spread the cards— maybe a hundred or more—across the big oak table, and asked the girls to pick one that spoke to them. This always worked well, because it was impossible to look at the sea of cards and not find one that jumped out with a story fast behind it.

Carla's writing was often such a tender counterpoint to the more dramatic narratives of the others; she'd picked a picture of autumn leaves.

As I walk to main building every morning I can't help but get lost as I stare at all the trees. Today coming out of the science building I saw the bright yellow gingko leaves thrown up against the bright blue sky and I had to stop and take it in.

Everyone pushed by me, basically sprinting to class as we always do here, but I couldn't move. I just can't understand how nature can create this breathtaking, saturated, organic wonder, and it goes unnoticed. I tried to take as many snapshots as I could in my mind and went on my way.

All I wanted to do was to get wrapped up in that beauty and stay

Carla

there; instead of learning about functions I wanted to make a leaf pile and jump in it over and over, trying to grasp these fleeting days of fall when I can, as the days get shorter and the darkness storms in before dinner.

I think Carla reminded me of Geoff; it was more and more because of him that it meant so much to me to do these groups with the Hotchkiss girls.

I drove home, took a shower, and tried to sleep.

The Gorilla Returns

The surgery seemed to have been a success, but it had been a long month since that last Hotchkiss/Touchstone meeting. I hadn't been able to think about much of anything but my back and its daily healing progress, if I even thought at all.

Touchstone had been far from my mind in those early weeks. But as I got a little stronger, and off medication, I began to think of meeting again, before the Hotchkiss girls went home for Christmas vacation. Nancy and Jess said okay, but wondered if I was really ready to do this.

I insisted I was.

John, who'd been my loving and attentive nurse as I healed, wondered too. But he drove me over with the cake I'd managed to bake for Miranda's birthday, and carried it in as I plodded beside him in my heavy brace.

The Hotchkiss girls greeted me with loving concern, handmade cards and hugs; their gratitude for my coming in before they left for Christmas vacation shone in their faces and gestures. Miranda, Molly, Ja'Keria, and Kimani all arrived with a staff person I had never met or seen before. Donna had had to work too many double shifts and hadn't been able to come in tonight.

Everyone sang and I cut big wedges of cake to hand around. But the Touchstone girls seemed uninterested, writing to the prompts I'd chosen without much spirit. Miranda was flat, almost bored, not appearing to care about the birthday celebration or the special gift I'd chosen for her, the silk bag embossed with butterflies she'd so admired at the Boston motel gift shop. Despite the warmth and enthusiasm of the Hotchkiss girls, when John picked me up I was deflated, consumed by the old shame at not being good enough.

The germs of Buddhist dharma I'd hoped I'd absorbed had vaporized, again.

I questioned myself. Could it be time to end this project, or would that be giving up?

Could saying no be saying yes to myself?

I didn't want to be another disappearing mother, foster parent, or clinician. I refused to cause the girls the combination of angst and emotional shutdown I'd so often seen when changes occurred in their lives. But was this projection, empathy, or even narcissism? Maybe a mixture?

My thoughts ran in circles.

Their lives were unsafe, in a constant state of flux. I would be adding to that if I left them.

I couldn't stand that.

But maybe they wanted to keep the drama, the spinning, they seemed to crave. That was safe and familiar, well-known to them. So was I trying to give the girls something they neither wanted or needed?

Was I doing this for them or for me?

I was looking at Pema Chodron's gorilla in the mirror again, flipping from one interpretation of my feelings to another, angry at myself for my confusion. I still thought of Touchstone as an eraser for my pain, not yet getting that it was that bridge to a new place, a cleaned-up, clearer-headed me.

My grief had lessened, there was no question about that. There were more and more times when I could take off its leaden coat, and I knew that was a result of being with these young women, writing with them, sharing in their lives. Immersing myself in their pain had given me distance from my own. Feeling their love for me had been nourishing. Giving to them had been giving to myself, as well.

Maybe I just needed better boundaries, I told myself, though I wasn't quite sure how to draw them. Less hugs? Fewer meetings? Not trying to make everyone happy?

Balance. I needed balance. I felt like I was teetering on one unsteady foot most of the time, at the brink of a needed new direction.

But I couldn't leave, not yet. I had come to define myself with this work. And honestly, now it was these Hotchkiss meetings I couldn't relinquish. I was told so frequently by the Hotchkiss girls how much they meant; I listened to their writing, saw their tears and what this space created for

I Am Not a Juvenile Delinquent

them in their stress-filled weeks. And they were so much easier than the Touchstone girls, so cooperative, eager and responsive.

I loved them. They too, had become "my girls."

But I couldn't do the Hotchkiss meetings without the Touchstone girls.

What to do?

Trapped

For Christmas, I'd gotten the girls each a $15 gift card from TJ Maxx. The roads were icy, so John offered to drive me to Touchstone, knowing I wanted to see the girls before their vacation, when some of them would be going home.

"Poor Miranda," I said to Donna. "She wrote a poem last week at Hotchkiss about another horrible experience—she doesn't seem to be doing well at all."

Donna agreed.

"Oh," I said, "That's right, you weren't at Hotchkiss with us last week—that new staff was—what's her name, I can't remember?"

Donna told me her name—Carol, I think it was—and looked at me sidelong—"but she's not with us anymore after what happened at Hotchkiss."

"What happened at Hotchkiss?"

"Oh, didn't you hear? Kimani stole a scooter, Ja'Keria stole some gloves off a Christmas tree in the hall, and all the girls were smoking. And I think someone stole some gum, too."

"Whaaat?" I was livid. "Those little shits!" I said.

"Didn't anyone tell you?" Donna seemed surprised.

"No, damn it," I said, "Why would I be reacting like this if I'd known?"

I was stunned, shocked, furious.

Clutching the bag of Christmas gift cards and typed poems from the weeks before, I tried to get calm and think straight about what to do as we entered the Lighthouse, another of the Touchstone dorms. There were no lights on and Molly was sitting on a chair, her head down, a black ski hat pulled over her blonde hair.

Molly got up to hug me. "Where are the other girls?" I wanted to know.

"Well, Kimani is off-grounds with some other residents, and Ja'Keria is upstairs sleeping. I think Dominique is taking a shower."

"Well, get them. What's this about Hotchkiss? I just heard."

Molly looked down. "I can't really talk about it. It's not fair. You should find out from someone else."

Helpless, crazed, I felt a mallet pounding at my chest.

"Can't anyone tell me what happened? Did Ja'Keria steal the gloves? She'd better get down here."

Molly went up to get her, but came back alone. "I kicked her bed but she wouldn't wake up."

"I came down today to give you girls Christmas gifts. I'm not giving one to Ja'keria if she stole something!"

I sounded childish to myself but I didn't care.

Donna told Molly she'd better get Ja'Keria down here, and Dominique as well. They both finally came downstairs, and a chastened Miranda walked in with a clinician. She looked so sad. I got up to hug her, clumsy in my heavy plastic brace.

"Can't someone turn on a light? It's so dark in here." I said, glaring at Ja'keria. "What's this about you stealing gloves from Hotchkiss?"

"I didn't take nothing, miss."

She repeated it and repeated it.

I told the girls how upset I was, about their disinterest in our poetry group today, about the theft I'd just heard of. Molly, Miranda, and Ja'keria wouldn't say anything about it. Donna was silent.

I felt bewildered, trapped in a torturous dream.

They were checked out, not listening to me, lost in their own personal swamps and defenses. Stupidly, not knowing what else to do, I gave each girl their gift card, and then returned all the typed poems I'd been working on for the last few days.

"Thank you, Sharon," all the girls said in a somber chorus. "Can we write today?"

"But it's so late, won't you be having dinner soon?

"We don't know."

Things seemed even more disorganized than usual. Everyone was behaving strangely, dancing around the truth. Or was my perplexity about exactly what had happened coloring my perceptions of their behavior?

More possibly, it was my inability to see that I was smack in the middle of an abusive situation.

I thought of my generous husband, waiting outside in a cold car. My skin itched under the uncomfortable brace. I was cold. I wanted to go home.

But I didn't do what I wanted to do.

Again.

"All right," I said. "Let's read the pieces that I've handed back, and we'll do a short write."

Compelled to give this scrambled meeting some normalcy, I read some poems from a Cave Canem collection called *Gathering Ground*. One told of a woman's reflections on her sister's pregnancy, another was *I'm A Fool To Love You*, by Cornelius Eady. I threw out prompts from the poems— the wrong man's kisses, pregnancy, being pregnant, sisters, a fool in love.

"Come on, we don't have much time," I said.

Molly wrote nothing, just sat droopily, the black hat almost covering her blue eyes.

"I'm not in the mood," she said.

At least Miranda wrote something, chilling as it was.

I'm a Fool to Love You

I fell in love with you
even before we met

I fell in love with the stories people told me
of how good you made them feel

I Am Not a Juvenile Delinquent

how you got rid of all their problems
it was at school where we met—

I remember it very well
we were behind the building—

you and me, and someone else
after a while my mom found out about you

about how I snuck you in the house
day after day after day

then you got me in trouble
I got arrested because of you

I got locked up
and I continued to love you

in every placement I've been in
we somehow have always come face to face

I keep getting hurt
you put me in bad situations

but I'm not going to stop
I'm not going to let you go

I will hold on to you
until the day I die

I don't care if you put me to my grave
I've never let you, drugs, go—

please don't ever leave

Tears burned behind my eyes. The room was cold. It was 6:45, night already.

"I've got to go," I said. "My husband is waiting for me in the car. I'll be back on the 5th, after vacation. Molly, will you still be here?"

She nodded. "Here until the 12th."

I handed her the Trinity essay she'd written with my comments, and a card with my phone number to call if she wanted more help with it or had questions. The girls got up, shuffled out.

Trapped

Glad I didn't have to drive home alone, I scrambled into our car, telling my husband about the thefts. His horrified response shocked me, pushed me to realize the immensity of this latest situation. It forced me to see that I was deep in murky water, my sense of clarity lost as I merged more and more with the girls and their dysfunctional residential facility and staff.

The fact that I hadn't been told seemed even worse than the thefts. This was my program, the Hotchkiss-Touchstone group. For six years, since the Black Box reading, we had built a trusting, strong connection that had been a tremendous success.

And now, this?

I was ready to end the whole project. But first, I had to deal with the disarray it had become.

* * *

I called Nancy the next day.

As always, she was calm and thoughtful in her response, such a relief to me. I told her I would speak with Beka, Touchstone's current director, about restitution, and punishment for the involved girls. We both thought that the most important piece of this was the violation of the group's trust. So, we'd meet with the Hotchkiss girls alone after vacation and tell them what had happened, then meet with the whole group and let them all talk about it.

We had a plan, and I felt her strong and wise support. At least I didn't have to tough this out alone.

John wisely continued to remind me that my not being told about this was big. Though I now felt drained and angry almost all the time, I made excuses for the girls and still didn't want to abandon what I saw as my commitment to them.

In denial of a larger reality, I remained attached to them, all the little me's who needed a mentor, a champion, a protector, a Sister Benedicta, as I had in my own adolescence.

* * *

I arrived at Beka's office on the third floor of the big house at 3:15, as planned. I'd suggested we, Donna, and the girls all meet to process the whole mess. Beka had no idea where the scooter was, but was willing to talk with someone at Hotchkiss, make restitution. However, she seemed strangely untroubled by the whole affair. It was only another one of the daily Touchstone crises to her.

I'd decided to write a letter to the girls explaining my feelings.

"I'm a writer, so it seemed like the best way to handle things," I told her, handing it to her for review. She read through it quickly—didn't say anything, just looked solemn.

Donna came in with Molly, Kimani, Dominique and another girl, both of whom were in the poetry group but not involved in the theft.

"Where's Ja'Keria?" I wanted to know.

"She's refusing to come," Donna said.

"How can she do that?" I wanted to know again.

Donna shrugged. "She's been impossible lately—refusing even to go to school."

Beka called Ja'keria at the Lighthouse and insisted that she be present. Ja'Keria continued to refuse.

She had too much power, I thought. It never would have been like this in my earlier years here.

"We'll just have to go ahead without her," I said, taking charge since Beka was not. Miranda had been off grounds—she'd gone AWOL again, and no one thought she was in shape for this group, so there would just be the four girls, Donna, Beka, and me. I handed the girls back their poems and notebooks, and said I had a letter to read to them about what had happened at Hotchkiss.

"Why are we meeting here?" Dominique wanted to know. "Why aren't we writing?"

"We're meeting here because what has happened is serious, girls, and Beka's presence as director is important. What happened at Hotchkiss was a big deal—nothing like that has ever occurred in the six years we've been doing the program there—it was a huge breach of my faith in you and the program."

I began to read the letter, telling them how betrayed I'd felt, what a wonderful, trusting history we'd had with the girls from Hotchkiss, and how they cherished their relationships with the girls of Touchstone. And how extra awful it would be if the stolen scooter was Carla's.

I told them that everyone has a bottom line, and that I'd hit mine.

Beka, aware of the group dynamics in a way I couldn't be while reading the letter, interrupted at this point to question whether everyone was listening and paying attention. Kimani had tuned out, absorbed with her notebook, looking down at the poems I'd returned. Beka quietly brought this to her attention. Kimani turned on her with a venomous look.

"I don't like you, I've never liked you, and I don't have to listen to you." She wrote some words on a piece of paper, pushed them towards Beka, and spoke the words she'd written.

"Fuck you, I hate you," Kimani said, toxins dripping from every syllable.

I drew back, stunned. I'd never heard any of the girls speak like this to a staff member, much less the director.

Beka then calmly suggested Kimani take a time-out.

"You don't know your own program," Kimani chillingly said. "We only need a time-out when we are escalating. I am not escalating."

Beka called for a staff to come and escort Kimani out of the meeting. I continued with the letter.

I suggested I might be mistaken about how they felt about our trips to Hotchkiss, that maybe they felt jealous and resentful when they saw how beautiful the school was and how privileged the kids were there. I acknowledged what a lousy hand life had dealt them, listing all the horrors they'd experienced, but that they had the chance and choice every day to try to move past their histories.

I talked about their talent and how I'd planned so many reading events for them because I wanted the world to hear their voices, but wondered if perhaps they didn't really want this gift from me. And I told them that I couldn't keep wanting for them if they didn't want for themselves.

I told them I was suspending the program indefinitely, of how important it was for me to be a role model for them in not continuing to allow myself to be abused by the current situation. I said we needed to make a fresh start with new girls when I decided it was time.

And I said we'd planned a meeting with Nancy and the Hotchkiss girls next week to discuss the theft and the trust it had broken, and I welcomed any feedback they had. I ended with the hope that we could turn this experience around and make a better beginning for us all.

Everyone was very quiet for a few minutes. Donna was the first to say something. She looked really upset. "I'm just learning to write," she said. "Don't stop now!"

"Writing is my life," Dominique said, "I will always write."

"Poetry group means a lot to us," the fourth girl said, looking sad and confused.

Molly stated that she had been in a tough personal place during that time, which, "though it was not an excuse" had led her to smoke and ignore the theft. "I think we should write a letter of apology, go to Hotchkiss and read it to the girls," she offered.

Beka said she needed to leave at a quarter to five, as she almost always did. I thought that was an unusual practice for the director of such an unstable community, but maybe it showed she had better boundaries than I did.

So the meeting ended with no resolution.

"We can meet again," Beka said. "That was a heavy letter you wrote. It will take some digesting."

I wasn't sure they'd gotten it, or wanted to. I knew the letter was wordy and long, emotional and definitely heavy, but I'd needed to write it, every word of it.

"Okay, Beka, let me think about this and we'll decide what the next step is."

I left her office and began walking down the stairs. I saw Miranda, back from wherever she had been, animatedly engaged in conversation with a staff member in the second floor hall. "Sharon!!" she yelled, and threw her arms around me. Molly was standing on the staircase too.

"I'm glad you didn't go to jail, Miranda. We need to talk." Molly said.

"Yes, Molly, you do—and tell her about the meeting, okay?"

I continued down the stairs and into the dark entrance hall, pushed open the heavy door. This was not the outcome I had expected. But then, that was true of almost every session I'd experienced at Touchstone.

A Family

Before the big meeting we'd scheduled the following week with the Touchstone and Hotchkiss girls, I snapped at John, stomped around the house and yelled at our dog, fretful and prickly.

Remember impermanence—I tried to tell myself—*bad things would pass too, right?*

Jess, Donna, Nancy, and Athena will all back me up, and the Hotchkiss girls will come through, I thought. Molly would too, and probably Miranda, if she was actually released to come. I didn't know about the others. Since Ja'Keria had refused to attend the meeting with Beka and was still in hot denial of her part in the theft, as was Kimani, I doubted either one of them would have made a positive contribution. Dominique was supposed to join us too, but it was unclear to me how she could help.

I received an email from Jess that morning, assuring me she and Donna would be there with as many girls as they could bring.

All the parking spaces were free at the main circle tonight, and I slipped into one. I walked down the long hall to the dining room. Nancy was waiting for me in the mostly-empty cavernous space, and she and I got a cup of tea and sat at a small round table in the back to wait for Athena. When she came in a few minutes later, she looked at me squarely and said, "How are you?" It wasn't meant in the offhand way that most people say it, not really expecting an answer, and if they got one, not listening or really caring. Athena cared. She really wanted to know how I was.

"Better than a while ago," I said. "This has been really devastating to me. It's been a mess at Touchstone—I just can't believe that no one told me about this, that I had to find out about it by accident. I think maybe I've hit my bottom with that place. Everything has gone so well for these six years with our group at Hotchkiss—I guess something was eventually bound to happen. Stealing. Damn. And honesty is so important to me—that's what all our writing is about—speaking the truth."

Athena looked at me compassionately as I spoke, shrugging off her pale blue quilted parka and white ski cap. Open, outspoken, she was in her early thirties, and so always had a different vantage point than Nancy and I did from which to view things. "Everyone steals stuff around here," she says. "We all steal things—in different ways."

Nancy began to speak about taking pencils, making copies, charging the second glass of wine on a business trip.

"But I am so scrupulously honest," I said—and then suddenly thought of some very big ways in which I had not been. I'd never actually stolen anything that I could remember—probably would have been too scared— but I had surely acted in ways that were not truthful. Maybe I was right now, not really looking directly at the reality staring me in the face, the big fat truth of how the girls had betrayed my trust in them and how I had been somehow rationalizing all of it so the programs in which I was so invested could continue.

But I didn't want to take philosophical reflections on honesty to the Hotchkiss girls tonight, help them make excuses for the Touchstone girls. I wanted them to take this news seriously, to feel the pain of it.

I wanted them to be a little hard on their friends.

"I guess we'd better get going," Nancy said. "Let's get dinner. The girls will be here soon." We took our plates to the private back dining room. Six girls had said they would join us. One would not be back until Thursday and three of the other girls were on a school trip.

I took a salad plate and some string beans, another cup of tea. The girls trickled in. Carla was the first to arrive. Becca. Caroline and Brady came next and then Lois. The private back dining room was inhospitably large, paneled in brown wood like the company boardroom to which many Hotchkiss students would eventually graduate. We clustered in a small group around a section of the large oak table. Becca was at the end, and Carla was across from me. Caroline was on the left, just out of my eye's reach. Lois sat next to me. No one knew the reason we'd gathered.

So I laid it out.

"Girls, something has happened in our Touchstone group that you need to know about. The last time the Touchstone girls were here for our meeting, some things got stolen." I explained the situation and added, "Say how you feel. Please feel free to say whatever you need to say, whatever comes to you. Okay?"

There was silence at first. Then Brady spoke.

"Touchstone" (the Hotchkiss girls called the group Touchstone, while the Touchstone girls called it Hotchkiss) "is our special place, our safe haven, the place where we can say anything and trust that we won't be judged. Now we will have to take a step back—but I think trust is still possible."

She seemed hurt, and unconvinced of the truth of her own words.

Caroline worried that it had turned things into a "we-they" situation and none of the girls wanted that—they loved the egalitarianism of our group. And without it, the group could not function the way it had.

Caroline had shown up at every meeting, writing very openly of her many questions and issues, and saying what many of the Hotchkiss girls told me they felt in the last piece she wrote before graduating :

> Touchstone lets me escape from the Hotchkiss bubble. Touchstone lets me escape the Hotchkiss stereotype. Touchstone lets me escape the frantic life I lead here. Touchstone lets me escape the tests, the quizzes, the homework, the sports, the parents, the friends, the enemies. Touchstone is a place to free the mind...to relieve stress...a safe haven, a place for us to tell the truth and not be judged. Touchstone is a dream.

I couldn't let the theft jeopardize such a prized situation for these girls. But it had.

I was glad that they were angry and hurt. Becca wanted to know why they couldn't have just asked us for what they needed, but then paused, seemed to know how shame would make such a question impossible. And maybe she realized that it wasn't need that had caused the thefts, but something else.

"Do you think the fact that this school is so lavish, has so much, could be an issue? I've often wondered about that. But it's just never seemed to be anything that bothered them...they have never expressed it as a concern, even when I've asked them."

I took another sip of my tea. I really wanted to know what they thought about this.

Becca stated, a bit defensively, that there were many kids at Hotchkiss who did not have a great deal. They were not much in evidence, though, many of us agreed.

Carla was twisting her hair into a knot, then letting it fall free; I knew this was hard for her.

"It's not your scooter, Carla," I said. "It has blue handles. Did you ever find it?"

"No, Sharon," she said. Her green eyes fixed on mine. "The Touchstone room is a sanctuary. It feels different now. I don't know if I'll feel the same again."

All of the girls had insightful things to say. But it was clear that none of them wanted to be in a position of judgment. That would have been antithetical to what this group had been in their lives.

Nancy and Athena didn't add much, but did take up the issue of theft at Hotchkiss—everyone agreed that it happened all the time—and that it wasn't necessarily germane to this discussion, although we did touch again on the various ways people could be dishonest. No one seemed to want to bail the girls out, though, to my surprise. I had expected that and was glad it was not happening.

"You need to tell them how you feel," I said, "it's important. We have created a family with this group, and as we would in a real family, we need to bring up all the hard stuff, put it out in the open and let everyone speak her truth. But you need to know too, that what you hear these young women reading every week is real—that almost all of them have been raped and/or sexually/physically abused, some by their own parents. When you hear their poems, you can forget that these things really happened to them—because it is so hard to take in the horror. Their lives have been hellish, though that is not an excuse for their behavior, just a way to comprehend it."

They were quiet for a few minutes. Maybe they were searching for a way to understand without destroying what they needed to be true, I thought.

"I just want to know how they did it," someone said. Someone else said, "I wonder where they smoked, and how someone didn't notice them."

"Well, we'll find out," I said. "Come on, let's go. They should be just getting here."

We all bussed our plates and walked down the hall to the classroom. It was empty. There were no pens or paper on the table, no cookies or pizza. We wouldn't be writing tonight, just talking. I was distressed that the Touchstone girls and Jess hadn't arrived. But I was sure they would come soon, as Jess was totally reliable.

Fifteen minutes late, but here, they walked in, Jess, Donna, Miranda, Molly, and Ja'Keria. Jess told us the others had refused at the last minute.

The Touchstone girls and I didn't hug in greeting as we usually did. There was no excited chatter, no effusive welcoming. Tonight, we were all grave and singular.

They walked into the room with their heads down and sat in a gloomy clump at the table. I opened the discussion by praising everyone for being here to deal with some tough things that had happened in our group, and said that the Hotchkiss girls had just been told the details. I said that Nancy, Athena, and I wanted this to be a conversation among the girls—although certainly Donna and Jess would and should contribute.

I repeated the idea that we'd become a family here, and that, after thinking about all the possible ways to deal with the situation, we had come up with this group process plan. I said that we wanted everyone to be able to speak her truth and come out feeling heard, that growth was possible through crisis and perhaps the group could be stronger than ever after this.

That I hoped so.

I may have sounded pompous, or too much like a therapist, but I didn't know how else to put it.

I needed to win this one, make it right. It was just too big.

• • •

Molly was wearing her black ski cap again. Looking miserable and tired, she spoke first. "We need to apologize," she said. "We smoked on the school grounds and know that is wrong. The scooter—we didn't take it—but we knew about it, didn't stop it, and didn't report it."

She stopped as if that was all she was going to say. Ja'Keria spoke next, said something along the same lines. Her voice was low and she seemed scared.

I saw Becca leaning over and whispering to Nancy, the pearl earrings that she always wore shining under her tangled brown hair. Nancy nodded. Becca spoke up. "I notice you are all sitting together," she said. "Why don't you move to places nearer to us in the circle?"

They obediently got up and moved. It was an icebreaker. Miranda sat next to Becca. Molly moved near to me. Everybody shifted in their seats—the prior formation had made it look like the Touchstone girls were on the witness stand and Hotchkiss was the judge. I was proud of Becca and relieved that the suggestion to move had come from one of the girls and not me.

Someone asked why the theft had happened. Since Kimani, who clearly was the specific culprit, wasn't here, my girls could only speculate. Kimani had evidently picked up the scooter outside, showed it to the other girls and put it in the back of the van before the staff person came out of the bathroom. She had taken the gloves defiantly, saying, "Well, if these are for poor families, I'm poor, and I'm taking some for myself."

Someone else posed the question about being overwhelmed by the grandness of the school—was that the reason?

"No, not at all," Miranda said. "We weren't overwhelmed. It was nothing that happened here or about you. It was all us." She wore her red jacket with the fur trimmed hood and the Chinese embroidery, never taking it off despite the fact that we were inside a warm room. Her dark hair was pulled up tight in a ponytail, and surrounded with a thick patterned headband.

Molly, looking down at the table, talked about the feeling that had been there that night for her; she said she just didn't care what she did. "I had a bad pass," she said simply.

Donna jumped in to tell us it had been her birthday that night and since she had worked double shift the day before, she'd wanted the night off.

"But maybe if I had been here…it wouldn't have happened." She looked sad and embarrassed.

Jess spoke up then. "It's not about the staff—although the girls took advantage of the staff that was on that night—it's about the girls and what they did. They need to take responsibility for it. It's hard, because the others who aren't here could say a lot more about what and why."

Becca wanted them to know that if they wanted anything, needed anything, they could always ask. Brady, her waist-length brown hair fastened into a ponytail, said what she had said in the dining room, that she would need to "take a step back" but was sure trust could be reestablished. She sounded more confident this time. Carla, serious face propped in her hands, expressed how important the group was to her, and how she hoped it would work again.

The others spoke of similar feelings. Nancy and Athena and I were unable to resist asking some more questions, like how did you do it and get away with it? Everyone wanted to know that.

They'd put the scooter in the back of the van when Carol was in the bathroom, they'd smoked over near the library and no one had said anything even though people had walked by and seen them. Clearly, Carol had been careless that night, not on top of the situation as Donna or Kaneisha would have been. I was sure that was the biggest reason they'd succeeded in the heist.

The feeling in the room was relaxed now, and everyone was talking. I turned to Jess.

"I think we need the Hotchkiss girls to come down and visit us at Touchstone—you've hosted us here so many times and they should see where we come from. We managed two visits in the last six years and they were such fun—sledding, and a pasta dinner in the Lighthouse—we need another one."

Jess made a small speech. "All the Touchstone residents are good kids, struggling with tough things, and they all are working as hard as they can to maintain. Touchstone is not a jail. It's a great place, and I am proud of my program and everyone in it." Her face reddened with the passion of her words.

She'd clearly given great effort to preparing for this meeting, and had executed it all flawlessly, as usual. I'd wanted her to see these special Hotchkiss girls, and how important this group was to them. Maybe she would go back and relate all this to the administration in a way I could not.

It was finally time to go. There was a feeling of solace in the room, of accomplishment. I went to speak with Nancy while the Touchstone girls lined up by the back table, ready to give big hugs to all, which they did. Molly was leaving on Friday, and Ja'keria was leaving sometime that week too. Miranda might still be here in the spring, but the embraces weren't about goodbye; they were about relief, forgiveness, compassion.

Molly sidled up, asking if I would come down in the next few days to say goodbye to her. Still feeling burned, I was hesitant. "Okay, I'll see what I can do, Molly. Maybe we can have lunch."

Jess was standing next to us. I asked her, "Could she be let out of school?

"Sure, Sharon, just let me know when and we'll set it up." I knew she would follow through.

Molly hugged me and they all left. I told her I'd call when I checked my schedule and the weather.

I wasn't at all sure I was going to go down to see her. I was still angry and hurt over the theft, the smoking and the lying, despite the good meeting we'd just had. Since I'd told the girls about reaching my bottom line, that I wasn't going to keep giving in the face of their lousy behavior, I'd been feeling raw and edgy, much less generous.

Maybe that was about some compassion for myself, finally. This was hard, a real habit change. But in ten years, I'd never felt the way I felt now, reluctant to give more.

I'd begun to realize I'd been kidding myself that I'd had no expectations, no hope for change, working here—of course I had. I'd wanted to matter in their lives. I'd wanted them to love me, the woman with the big hole in her heart, make that hole a little smaller. And in another hidden subtext, I'd hungered to redeem my lonely adolescent self.

I wanted to spring us all out of prison and into freedom with my magic, the magic of writing. I'd wanted to change the world, their worlds, my world, the world of our bigger communities, with our loud, wild voices.

I'd wanted to be a Sister Benedicta to them, but a wiser, more proactive one, who grasped the realities of their lives and of her own, and operated from those, not from some idea of a distant God's cool embrace.

Molly

It was January 2009, and Molly had been at Touchstone almost a year. After years of drug abuse and running away, she'd stolen her mother's car and credit card, high on drugs, drove to New York with friends just as high as she was, bought clothes and food, got lost in the Bronx and ran out of gas. After trying to use the card at a convenience store, she'd split when the card came up as stolen. Somehow they'd all made it back home. Her mother had wisely pressed charges.

Probably she'd weighed less than 100 pounds, eyes sunk deep into a hollow face, matted hair, dirty clothes. I'd seen the picture the Touchstone nurse had taken of her then, a wake-up call to show Molly when she deviated from the program. After her arrest, she had to detox in detention on only two Tylenol every six hours for three days. In one of her poems, she'd written about how she shook and vomited and cried and writhed for those three days on the hard cement floor of her cell. After that, she'd been sent to us. It was either Touchstone, which the judge considered a kind of rehab, or a ten-year bid at York CI, she'd told me.

One sunny afternoon, sitting down at the Lighthouse, she told me that she'd actually considered the jail bid seriously.

"Why, Molly?" I asked, incredulous.

"Because it's so easy to get drugs there. I could have kept using."

Now, if she violated parole, she'd go straight to jail for those ten years. No college in DC or anywhere else. She insisted she was not going to. But I knew drug abuse was a chronic disease and relapses were always part of it. I knew there was a strong chance Molly would have one sooner rather than later. She loved drugs and was ambivalent about recovery.

Because I'd really wanted to see her and have a chance to talk before she left, I overcame my testiness and decided to take Molly out on Wednesday. As promised, Jess arranged things with the staff so this could work, and I picked her up at the big stone house at 12:30. She bounced out the door laughing. "Yay, out to lunch! I'm leaving!"

She was wearing dangly silver hoops and at least six gold circles in each ear. She'd streaked her blonde hair brown on her last pass home and pulled it back with a clip. Molly actually cared about how she looked now. When she'd first come to poetry group, she hadn't. Her hair was never washed, her clothes were always dark. She was thin now too, but it was becoming, not the unnatural thinness of the coke addict.

"Where do you want to go?" I asked, as she slid into the front seat of my car and immediately turned on the radio.

"Anywhere," she said. I headed to Litchfield center.

"Aspen Gardens," I said. "Okay?"

"Sure," she said. "I don't care."

We walked in, went to a booth in the corner. I remembered sitting here with Jeni years ago, eating ice cream on a summer night. Molly reminded me a little of Jeni, the rare middle-class white girl at Touchstone. *They always seemed to have the most serious offenses,* I thought. If a young woman of color had done what they had done, she'd have gone straight to York CI, not to the much less restrictive environment of Touchstone.

* * *

Molly and I looked at the menus—we wanted to figure out what to order before we settled down to talk. "Should I get the calamari or the shrimp and artichoke pasta?" she asked, having a more sophisticated palate than the other girls.

"Whatever you want," I said. "Get whatever you want."

She chose the shrimp. I got chicken souvlaki. She told me she'd become a vegetarian since being at Touchstone and that's why she'd lost weight. "But I eat fish," she asserted.

She asked how my back was doing, wanted to know what pain pills I took for it.

"Oxycodone," I told her. "But I hardly took any, I hated them, hated the way they made me feel, like I wasn't really here. I've still got a half-bottle, and more from the dentist when I had a terrible infected tooth at Christmastime."

Molly

"Oh my god, Sharon, you can sell those for $25 a pill. Give them to me to sell—I'll give you a cut." She got a dreamy look on her face.

"Yeah, sure, Molly. Look at the headlines that would make—'Writing teacher gives Touchstone resident narcotics to sell. Both go to jail.' "

"Yeah," she smiled.

"Wow, you must have felt good with those," she said.

"Molly," I said, "those pills were meant to block the pain from my surgery, not for getting high. I didn't feel good, just out of pain, and yes, a little zoned out. But when I had that infected tooth, they hardly touched it. They don't work with nerve pain."

"Well," she said, "you have to snort it—it works better that way. Take the pill and rub it with paper towels to get the coating off—that's bad for you—then crush it into a powder and snort."

"How do you snort?" I asked, curious. I had learned so many things since working at Touchstone that I would never otherwise have known— what a lap dance is, where to hide a gun, places you can stay if you run away from home, how to light a crack pipe, that you can earn five dollars a minute by stripping in front of a webcam.

She took a yellow Splenda packet from the white china container on the table—rolled it up and mimicked the snorting action.

"I'd mess it up, "I said, laughing. "I'd get the powder all over the place."

"Well," she said helpfully, "you can rub cocaine on your gums. It numbs them out completely."

"Where am I supposed to get cocaine?" I said.

"From me," she said, and her eyes twinkled. We both laughed.

It didn't occur to me that she might be speaking the truth.

The waitress brought her salad, a yellow plastic basket of fluffy bread, my watery decaf. Molly had told me a doctor informed her that if she went back to drugs she'd live at most eighteen months. She could choose that path, easily. She'd let me know that she never expected to live past twenty-one. I knew she was feeling good, now—the flush of eleven months of a world protected from drug abuse and boundaried by parole and the threat of jail, good friends and connections made in sobriety. And I was well aware that when she got home, back with her mom and school and friends, that this all could change, and very fast, parole or no.

What I didn't know was that she was still using, on pass, the weekends home the girls earn by good behavior.

"Molly," I asked, "have you decided if you're going to live or die? What do you think?"

"I don't know."

"What's heroin like, Molly? I want to know what it is that pulls you so strongly. Is it like an orgasm? Tell me."

She paused, rolled her eyes, tapped her fingers on the plate of half-finished pasta. "I don't know, Sharon…well, imagine you are all cozy in your bed, wrapped close in a down comforter, and you never have to get up, you can just stay there and drift…" She got that dreamy look on her face again.

She told me how much she and her mother clashed, how she could control herself with everything and everyone else but her. She told me about an after-school job working at a bowling alley that she'd start when she got home. I asked if she would divulge more about the bad pass she'd been so depressed about the day I came down with Christmas presents. She told me she'd had to do a "1-36" (a police report) on a boyfriend, that he had raped her.

We were both quiet after those words. I was used to hearing the girls tell me such horrors, but they never failed to disturb and upset me.

"You have awful guys in your life," I said.

"Yeah, I know. Gotta do something about that."

"Why don't you try a girl?" I said, half-joking. "Everyone else at Touchstone is doing it—gay for the stay, as they say."

"I did, and she got AIDS. She started getting sick and went and got tested. HIV. I got tested too. No AIDS. We didn't do anything after that, but I stayed with her until she died. You know, Sharon, my poem, *These Are My Friends*? She's one of those. So many of my friends have died. I lost another one a few weeks ago. She left rehab, overdosed and slit her wrists. Dead. Another one, dead."

Molly ordered some ice cream after asking me if it was okay. "Of course," I said. "Of course it's okay." The waitress brought two spoons. I scooped some of the coffee ice cream into my decaf.

We talked about her father. He was an alcoholic, pot smoker, whose longtime live-in girlfriend was a substance-abuse counselor, as she had mentioned in one of her poems. Go figure. He'd put beer into Molly's sippy cups.

"My mother was furious about that." she said.

"As well she should have been, " I said.

"My father abused me. My sister too."

She told me it happened until she was ten, that her mother knew and that she thinks he went to jail for a while. That she hated having to go to his house for weekends. I urged her to talk with her mother about her anger over this, but Molly said she wasn't going there.

The waitress brought our unfinished lunches in square Styrofoam containers. The coffee ice cream was melting in its stainless steel bowl.

"Your mother must be happy about you going to college. Being a teacher and all."

"No, she isn't. She doesn't want me to go, and she's not going to pay for it."

Her mother was not supporting her going to college? I was incredulous.

"How about your father?"

"Nope. They wouldn't pay for my S.A.T. s either. I finally got the $45 out of my father by saying I would pay it back."

"But why, Molly?"

"I don't know why."

"Don't you talk to Vernell about all this?" Vernell was her Touchstone therapist and had met with both parents. Now I was wishing I'd had this talk with Molly earlier, way before she was just ready to leave. Maybe I could have—what? No, I probably couldn't have done anything.

"Yeah."

"Well, make her do more, deal more with them on this college stuff. You've gotten your life together, you're smart, you're talented. You're clean. It's the next step."

"They don't want me to go to DC. My uncle is there. Like I told you in Boston, I'm going to live with my best friend. We've been planning this for years. She's going to school to become a PA. Even if I don't get into Trinity, I'm still going to college. I will go to a community college. I will pay for it all myself. I'll do it on my own."

I could hear and see that she was determined. But she was here, in a restaurant with me, going back to a residential treatment program in a half-hour, not yet back in the world.

She went on. "I don't need my mother. I have Amy." (A staff member at Touchstone). "I have you. I have my friends."

"Molly, what is your mother's first name?" I suddenly wanted to know her mother's name.

"Audrey, why?"

"Audrey, " I said to the air in the restaurant. "I know this girl has disappointed you badly, let you down countless times. But she wants to connect. She needs you."

Molly looked at me strangely.

"Sorry, Molly, I am just so upset. I want your mother to hear you, see you, support you."

"It's okay, Sharon, I can handle it."

Blood on the Floor

After returning from Hartford Hospital, where I'd gotten a shot in my shoulder for the biceps tendinitis I'd gotten from all the typing, I decided to call Molly. She'd been home for a while, and we'd had tentative plans to meet on Sunday when I would be driving back from visiting my grandchildren in the Boston area. But I hadn't heard from her.

I was always anxious when she didn't return my calls, thinking she'd had a slip since she'd been back living with her mom and sister. And after dinner with Miranda last week, I already knew she had.

I'd taken Miranda to Aspen Gardens after interviewing ten girls for the poetry group. No one but Jess knew it yet, but I'd finish with this one last session. I'd complete the school year, with four Hotchkiss meetings, a reading and talk I'd been invited to do at Sacred Heart University in Fairfield with the girls, and end with the poetry festival, after which I planned to retire from Touchstone for good.

The Hotchkiss caper had been devastating, the proverbial last straw. It had forced me to see my burnout, that I'd been in a state of continual stress for far too long.

That I had to give up hope that things would improve was finally clear to me.

It would be a divorce, really. I'd heard somewhere that any good love affair left blood on the floor. The hurt feelings, the disappointments, the betrayals, were part of that blood, but my love for this work and the girls were the body from which they spilled.

My mind had finally settled.

I'd met with Beka for a half-hour before the interviews with the new girls to tell her I was leaving.

"Are you going to do that reading? What is it called...?"

"You mean Artwell?" I said.

"Yes, Artwell," she said. "I hope you will do that again."

"No, "I said, feeling remnants of ambivalence churn in my heart. "I can't. It's too stressful. And the girls won't be ready, we're getting a late start and only a few of them have work to read."

"Is there a way we can help?" She gazed at me with unusual concern.

"Not really," I said. "There's a huge address list to get out, invitations would have to be designed, and the posters would need to be distributed—but that's the smallest part. Having the material for a show is the big piece. We won't have it. And besides, so much always goes wrong at the last minute, we are all way too anxious. I just don't think I can do it this year."

I struggled not to capitulate.

I'd gotten chewed on by my Touchstone work, yes. But I'd bandaged my bitten skin and gone back, over and over. I'd toughened my hide with the knotty tissue scars made.

And it had been so much better than if I'd been in a therapist-client relationship with the girls. I had been able to take them out to eat, bring them to Boston, to readings and performances with them as stars. I'd been able to hug them, bake them cookies and birthday cakes, give them teddy bears. I'd been given so many opportunities to practice my Buddhist beliefs in impermanence, lowering expectations, wise choices, accepting things are they were.

And that's what I was doing now. Walking across that bridge of acceptance. And because of the constant rehearsals in surrender that Touchstone had demanded, I saw that, after twenty-two long years, I was no longer clinging so tenaciously to the grief that had lodged in my heart and body after Geoff died.

Oh, it was still there, always would be, waiting in the background to knock me over with an unexpected triggering. But that grief was no longer my constant companion. I'd learned to carry it differently, to let go of its insistent demand to inhabit every moment of my daily life. The girls had taught me, reluctant learner that I'd been.

Yes, it had been all about the girls. No matter what Touchstone staff and administration thought, said or didn't say, it didn't matter.

The girls had been what mattered.

The Perfect Teachers

At Aspen Gardens for our dinner together, Miranda ordered a hamburger, French fries, onion rings and a Pepsi. I got a tuna sandwich and decaf in a thick white mug. Her current hairdo was long bangs, with two short bunches in the back, big hoop earrings. Her hair was so jet-black it looked dyed.

She had an exotic look, and always wore tight-fitting jeans and low-cut tops that set it off. It was a curse, really, for her, to be so beautiful and appealing, to have such a lovely body. Men and boys were instantly drawn to her because of it, and her ability to resist their advances was minimal, especially when the liaisons involved drugs.

She picked at her French fries, dunking them heavily in ketchup.

"Tell me about Hotchkiss," I said. "What really happened? I haven't gotten a straight story from anyone."

"Carol" —the staff member—"went to the bathroom so we could smoke. Molly and I went first, behind the main building. Ja'Keria and Kimani stole the scooter and the gloves while we were smoking and put them in the van—we didn't see them until she stopped at the gas station. Everyone told a different story—we tried to cover for each other. I'm a terrible liar—everyone knows when I'm not telling the truth. It was a mess."

"How did they get the scooter into the dorm?"

"Oh, easy. Carol searched me and Molly and they said they wanted to go down to the Lighthouse to say goodnight to somebody. I think they left it there."

"A scooter is such an odd thing for a Touchstone girl to have—so preppy— it's just so surprising that no one noticed it."

"Hmm, yeah, I don't know. Jake said something to me a few days later in the kitchen about it and I said oh yeah, we were smoking—they didn't even know that, he was asking about the scooter—I should have kept my mouth shut."

I Am Not a Juvenile Delinquent

"Tell me about the Percocet last weekend," I said. "Why?" She had sniffed a bunch of it again and had had to go to the ER while on pass.

She shrugged again. "Nothing to tell. Someone gave it to me and I wanted it."

"Do you think you're an addict, Miranda?" I asked.

"No, no way!" She smiled.

"Would Molly say you were an addict?"

This gave her pause. "Yes, I guess..."

"And Molly—she's definitely an addict." I said. Miranda nodded in agreement. "I worry so much about her using again. The stakes are so high. Do you think she is?"

Miranda suddenly became very uncomfortable, looking everywhere but into my eyes, giggling nervously, pulling at the fur on the hood of her white jacket.

"Well, I guess I've got my answer."

"I told you I couldn't lie. Don't tell her I told you, don't tell her, Sharon!"

"I'm sure she'll tell me, Miranda."

• • •

And she did, as I rode up the Mass Pike to Boston talking to her on my cell phone, making plans for our visit on Sunday.

"Sharon, I had a dirty urine last Friday."

"Oh, no, Molly! What was it? I can't remember the one that lasts a long time—is it pot or cocaine?"

"Oh, that's pot. Mine was cocaine—three to five days. They caught me this time."

"You mean you've been doing it all along?"

"Yeah, a few weeks after I got home—it's so stressful, Sharon, the job, school, being home, my mother..."

"Yes, but how about Nar-Anon, and that friend's mother who was going to support you...you need support to stop, you know that."

The Perfect Teachers

"I just don't have time, Sharon."

"Molly, it's college. It's ten years in jail. And remember that doctor who said if you went back to drugs you'd be dead in eighteen months?"

"Yeah, I know. But I think I'm invincible."

I sighed to myself. Of course she did, everyone at that age did. Geoff certainly had.

"Well, you're not. None of us are. I don't want to visit you in jail, Molly."

"I'm trying, Sharon. My P.O. gave me another chance 'cause I'm doing so good. But next time..."

"You have to do more than try, you need support. Touchstone wasn't a rehab. You needed a rehab. You need one now."

"I know."

"Does your mother know?"

"I had to tell her."

"How did she react?"

"Just like my mom."

"What does that mean?"

"Like she thought I'd fail—like, not surprised."

"Well, are we going to meet on Sunday?"

"Yeah, but I don't get my work schedule until Saturday night, so I'll have to call you. I think we should meet at the Starbucks in Mansfield, okay?"

● ● ●

John dropped me off about 3:30 so we'd have time before she had to leave to get to work by 6:00. He had been such an anchor for me in the turmoil of my years at Touchstone, always understanding how much it meant to me to do this work, though I'd probably complained more about the bad stuff than told him about the good. He'd come to every one of our events, and the girls loved and fussed over him. I'm not sure I would have lasted as long as I had without his backing. And he was backing me now in this new place, having known long before I did that it was time for me to leave, but waiting for me to see it on my own.

When I walked in, Molly spotted me immediately. She looked so thin, her long blonde hair under the black ski cap she used to wear at Touchstone all the time. *It's the cocaine*, I thought. *That's why she's so thin.* There was an older woman with her, in a green chamois shirt and khakis, brown hair pulled back, wire-rimmed glasses.

"My mother wants to meet you," Molly said, and the brown-haired woman moved forward to clasp my hand.

"I am so happy to meet you at last," she said. "I am so grateful for all you have done for Molly, you have been wonderful to her, helped her so much."

I put my arm around Molly and drew her close.

"I love her, she's a really special girl."

Molly's mom reached up behind her glasses to wipe her eyes. "Mom, are you crying?" Molly asked with surprise.

"Yes, I am."

I was surprised too. Audrey neither looked nor acted like anything I had been prepped by Molly to expect. We went on to have a lively conversation about my alma mater Trinity, where Molly'd been accepted with full scholarship, and how similar it was to the small women's college she'd gone to in upstate New York. She wanted Molly to live in the dorm for her first year, to help with the stress.

"No way, I'm not going to so forget it, Mom."

I decided to change the subject. "Aren't you a Montessori teacher?" I asked.

"Mom, would you leave, please?" Molly said impatiently.

"Okay, just call me twenty minutes before you're ready to come home, okay?" She turned to me. "There's no way you can take her home, you'd get hopelessly lost."

"Okay," I said, hugging her goodbye.

"I'm starving," we both said in unison, and stood in line to get sandwiches and coffee.

"I've got money," Molly said, waving some bills.

"Don't worry, I'll cover it."

We took our coffee and food to two big green velvet chairs in a corner and sat down, hungrily eating the hot mushroom and cheese sandwiches. "Your mom is nothing like I thought she'd be—so different-looking from you, I'd never know you were mother and daughter."

"Yeah, I look like my dad."

"Molly, I'm so worried about your dirty urine. I've been thinking, since we talked on the phone—if you get another one, you need to go to rehab, not jail! You need to tell your probation officer that."

"I already did, Sharon. He says there is no protocol for that, I'd just have to do rehab in jail."

"That is so stupid, you're not a criminal, you're a drug addict, and you need help to quit, not jail. How about rehab right now? You've finished your course work to graduate and have time before college."

"Can't do it, I'm on parole." She settled way back in her chair, and I got up to move mine so I could see her better.

"I know I need it, though."

"What about Nar-Anon and your friend's mom?"

"Yeah, I'm going with her to Hartford this week. I'm trying, Sharon, I really am."

"Why Hartford, why not here?"

She looked at me like I was crazy. "All the dealers are here—everyone I know. I've gotta get out of here—Willimantic is the heroin capital of Connecticut!"

"But there will be drugs wherever you go—certainly in DC."

"Yeah, but I won't be able to get them as easily as I can get them here—all I have to do is pick up the phone and I get direct delivery..."

"Oh, Molly. Why? I've read so many books on drugs—drug users—I know self-control doesn't work, but it's so hard to believe—what is it that pushes you to make such a bad choice when everything else is so good for you right now?"

"When I get that craving, it's almost a sick feeling in here." She put her hand on her stomach. "I just have to have it."

I was powerless, just as powerless as she was, and I hated it. But this time, I refused to be eaten by the cannibals. Tarray had given me crucial lessons I hadn't heeded. Molly was offering me more. I thought she'd use again, get caught, go to jail.

My impotence stood there like a boulder between us. Her body felt so thin as I hugged her goodbye, her eyes close to hollow. There was absolutely nothing I could say or do that would make a difference. I had a glimmer of understanding now, of her mother's burden, the drug addict's burden, of mine—the whole huge millstone of life.

Conclusion

This Is The Way It Is Right Now

At some point in my ten years at Touchstone, I wrote this poem, the only one I have ever been able to write about the girls.

Creed

I believe in the daughter I never had
how she multiplies in front of me every Tuesday
in black and brown and caramel tan
I believe in her arms, the arms she shows me
again and again, crisscrossed with razor cuts
why I say, why and she says because when the blood
comes out the pain comes out, and I believe her
and I believe in her crazy hair, woven into braids
shaved off completely or just wild black stuff sticking up
I believe in her pen moving across the paper
screaming her life out in ink, her story of a mother
who sold her for drugs at five, mother and dealer
holding her down and I believe in the incredible
indelible damage done to her and I believe
that she and the girl who always sits next to her
(one day I bent down to pick up a dropped pen
saw their feet touching under the table) I believe
they love each other—what passes for love
in their ripped up hearts—but I also believe
that it will be over soon and badly and I will see
wretchedness on their faces and they won't sit
together any more—I believe in her hugs
and how those hugs reach the huge holes

in both our hearts—I believe in her skin-tight jeans
uptowns and tank tops, her quilted black jacket
with fur-trimmed hood, the bright hoop earrings
with her name—Shanique, Bianca, Xiomara, Tarray,
Chimere, Melanie, Shamecca, La Shanna—
spelled out in twisted gold plate—I believe in her
walking down the hill to meet me, in her walking away
and forgetting me—I believe in her short attention span,
her desire for chocolate chip cookies (with macadamia
nuts, please, miss), M&Ms, pizza and chips—I believe
in her hope, a thing with feathers as Emily said
feathers that beat hard inside sometimes and flutter
sometimes and I believe in her yearning for kisses
for drugs, for sex and new clothes and I believe
in her triumphs—beating heroin for three months
a prize-winning poem—her mother calling—I believe
in her excitement at a pregnancy at fifteen—"now
I'll have a child who will give me the love I never had—"
and I believe in her despair and confusion when it finally
sinks in that giving birth is going to hurt and give her
stretch marks, that diapers and formula cost money,
that she can never go back—and I believe in her hopeless-
ness,
though now that I have told you that I believe that I wanted
to finish with hope, her hope, my hope,
but I believe that I can't

Touch: A Journal of Healing, Issue 3, January 2010

A story like this *should* finish with hope, shouldn't it? Redemption for me, bright new worlds for the girls, whose lives have been gloriously transformed by the poetry groups they attended at Touchstone?

Before Geoff died, I'd spent much time dreaming another version of myself—my childhood cancelled, a shiny new version in its place, created by the hard work of therapy, Buddhist practice, shamanic intervention, a young girl's prayers, the cadence of loss and longing no more singing in my soul.

I'd imagined I was powerful enough to make aspirations, my own and those of others, into reality.

But the catastrophe of his death presented me with a consummate reckoning, the face of Pema Chodron's gorilla in the mirror, the place where I had no choice but to embrace what was happening to me or push it away.

Perhaps I'd hoped I could confront it by my years of working at Touchstone, in encouraging others to speak the truths of their lives by offering my own thorny veracity. Perhaps I'd hoped by doing that, I'd help the girls look into their own mirrors and welcome what they saw.

And perhaps I had, to some extent.

But the girls taught me hope was dangerous.

I'd discovered that to be fully alive and awake to life is to be continually thrown out of the nest. That controlling my experience was impossible. That throwing the kerosene of wanting things to be different from how they were, on my anxiety, grief, and anger only made things worse. That's how I saw the idea of hope now, not as a wish or dream, nor the idea that things could magically morph into a more desired outcome without effort or intention on my part.

That didn't make sense to me anymore.

And I'd discovered too, another species of love—real love—my own capacity for giving and receiving it expanded by being with the whole, hurting, beautiful selves the girls presented to me week after week, year after year.

In the years after I left, I've found new places to stumble and learn and grow, time to grasp and digest and breathe in the beauty and anguish of all those poems, all their life stories, all the memories of our sessions and readings and road trips, disasters and triumphs, and best of all, space in which to rest and not try so hard all the time.

I've wondered how I'd have dealt with Geoff's death and my grief, all those years at Touchstone and Hotchkiss, if I'd been able to absorb those truths back then. But really, I'd known at some level, somewhere in my deepest self, that I'd needed this bridge to it, this long-term, tangible, hands-on experience of loss and powerlessness, the knowledge that suffering began

I Am Not a Juvenile Delinquent

to dissolve when we could question the belief that there was anywhere to hide. There was a process that had to be navigated, through many unskillful choices, poor judgments, that could wake us up, finally, to some wisdom. To accepting things as they are, not how we want them to be. To see that gorilla in the mirror and smile with affirmation, acceptance and yes, even love.

It was so strange to think of throwing out hope as a relief, but that's how I felt.

I have this big family of daughters now, out there in the world, struggling to stay straight, to stay sane, to keep their men, their jobs, their welfare checks, care for their children, the daughters and granddaughters I never had. And it's good, and I'm glad I had the tangled gift of those ten years.

They've cast off their labels and walked into the fullness of themselves. And I too have relinquished mine, mother of a dead son.

Across the bridge at last, I'm moving on now, not away, really, but deeper in, somehow, to the new place I can go to in myself, tamed of my wild grief, my impatience and need, quieter, more tranquil, more of the woman I have always wanted to be.

Afterword

Trauma. It usually starts in childhood, orchestrated by those we blindly trust and love. As we read each of Sharon's girls' poems, we are gifted to see the strength and tenacity in each of them. Their ability to survive, hope...to simply live.

We can learn a lot from these young women; these girls society falsely claim to be "delinquents." As an audience member at one of the girls' readings responds, it is "[their] graceful dignity and surviving ambition to be better than what they had faced [that] is like a candle in a dark room that got brighter with each girl's voice and words..."

We all have a "gorilla [staring back at us] in the mirror"—how we decide to face the gorilla is the ultimate test of our capacity to hope, survive, live... accept, in the darkest moments of our lives.

In *I Am Not a Juvenile Delinquent*, Sharon Charde shows us the light that is in all of us, and in all things, if we are ready to see it.

DONNA HYLTON
New York, New York

●　●　●

Donna Hylton is the author of *A Little Piece of Light. A Memoir of Hope, Prison and a Life Unbound*. She was incarcerated in Bedford Hills Prison for Women for twenty-seven years, during which she earned multiple degrees. Since her release in 2012, her work has focused on building communities through economic, racial, and gender justice, and the correlation between sexual violence and abuse and victim trauma and response.

Acknowledgments

For *I Am Not a Juvenile Delinquent* to have come this far feels little short of miraculous to me. After many years of my attempts to find a home for it, a friend suggested Mango Publishing, and I immediately sent off yet another query letter to them. A few days later, I heard from my now-editor Natasha Vera, asking for a proposal. The rest is glorious history. Natasha has shepherded me valiantly through the many challenges a first author faces, and I am so grateful to her as well as the very robust marketing team at Mango. They really know their book-selling strategies well, and my appreciation for everyone there abounds.

But for the girls, this book of course would never have been written. There are so many of them at both Touchstone and Hotchkiss who cannot be personally named here, but know you are loved and thanked from my deepest heart. Tarray, Chimere, Jeni, Ellie, Tiffany, Mayra, Joy, Marissa, Melanie, Miranda, Molly, Inny, Artrese, Dominique, Ja'Keria, Rontae, Shontia, Natalia, Davina, Octavia, Bianca, Xiomara, Shanique, Jessica, Carla, and Becca, none of you have ever left me. Some of you will find yourselves and your poems in *I Am Not A Juvenile Delinquent* and I am thrilled that the world will hear your voices. But without fantastic Touchstone staff Lesley Budny, Lori LaLama DeVito, Michelle Sarofin, Jen Cowell Block, Jana Winston-Wu, Donna Thomas, Jess Clow, Kaneisha Hill, and Karen Fletcher, I never would have been able to get you all to our many performances, indeed even our weekly meetings. A special thank you to Lori for believing I could do this and championing me despite pushback. To Dr. Yitzhak Bakal and the North American Family Institute, more appreciation, for continuing to keep the door open for me.

To Nancy Gaynor and Athena Fliakos, enormous thanks for doing what it took to get and keep our Hotchkiss program going, and to Sarah Tames, for starting it all. To Sister JoAnn, thank you for telling me that Touchstone existed and to "just do it," and Gayle Brooks for all her support from DCF. Gratitude to Michele Murdock for giving me the wonderful Carol Henderson, my first editor, to Martha Toll for enormous and continuing support, to Nancy Manter, Peter Seward, and Jo Eldredge Morrissey for cover art and photo contributions. Julie Fowler, you have always supported me and the girls, and Alison Meyers and Pam Nomura, what an incredible trip we took together with Tarray, Fresh Voices, and the Hartford Academy. The Monday Poets were there for me in the beginning of this journey and I'm so grateful for that, as well as for all the brilliant women poets who came to our festivals, and the many women who've come to my writing groups over the years. And to Stewart Wilson, thank you for hosting our Artwell readings.

Jon Baskin, how brave you were to come up from the city and make the moving film, *I Am Not a Juvenile Delinquent*, documenting all of us and the work in a way nothing else could—tremendous thanks.

Clara Rosemarda, Douglas MacDonald, Annie Nugent, and Kamala Masters kept me on the path when I faltered and helped me to learn "this is the way it is right now," whether I liked it or not. To Sarah Getz and Nancy Causey, yoga teachers par excellence, my gratitude for helping me to stay as strong as I've needed to be.

Tremendous thanks to Natalie Goldberg and her Taos workshops where "writing practice" all began, and to Polly Raye, who never takes no for an answer. To Backwaters Press and Greg Kosmicki, who published *Branch In His Hand*, and gave me so much courage to keep going, I am forever grateful. Barbara Kathe, you knew me when. Sara Warner-Phillips, who magically appeared from the past offering much-needed redesign of my website, thank you. Livio and Wendy Pestilli, I love you forever. Francesco Lombardi and Suore Lucia, *abbracci e baci*. To all my dearest residency friends, how much your encouragement, support, and fellowship has helped me persevere.

The MacDowell Colony, the Corporation of Yaddo, Virginia Center For Creative Arts, and Vermont Studio Center have fed, housed, sheltered, and supported me with many treasured residencies at which I did much of the writing and revising of this book. I have been so fortunate to have had the privileges they gave me, and am so grateful for them.

Hedi, Nick, Aidan, and Max have enriched my life with their presence and love. Thank you, dear daughter-in-law and cherished grandsons.

My beloved sons, Matthew and Geoffrey, I couldn't imagine life without you, but then I had to. Matthew, the son who lives, for how you have helped me survive, there are no words big enough for my gratitude and love for you. Geoffrey, you continue to inspire me and the world from your existence somewhere not far away, I think. And my husband John, the steady, calming, loving presence, who has read every word I've written, attended every reading the girls gave, as well as all of mine, who unfailingly supports me in all I do, you are the best Buddha a girl could have, and I don't tell you enough how much I love you.

About the Author

Sharon Charde practiced family therapy for twenty-five years and has led writing groups for women since 1992. She has won numerous poetry awards, has been widely published in literary journals and anthologies, and has been nominated seven times for the Pushcart Prize. The BBC adapted her work for an hour-long radio broadcast in June 2012, and she has six published collections of poetry.

From 1999 to 2016, she volunteered at a residential treatment facility teaching poetry to adjudicated young women, creating a collaborative group with a local private school for eleven of those years. Sharon has been awarded fellowships to the Vermont Studio Center, Virginia Center for the Creative Arts, The MacDowell Colony, the UCross Foundation, and The Corporation Of Yaddo. She lives in Lakeville, Connecticut, with her husband John and the fifth of their black Labs, Stella.

Mango Publishing, established in 2014, publishes an eclectic list of books by diverse authors—both new and established voices—on topics ranging from business, personal growth, women's empowerment, LGBTQ studies, health, and spirituality to history, popular culture, time management, decluttering, lifestyle, mental wellness, aging, and sustainable living. We were recently named 2019's #1 fastest growing independent publisher by *Publishers Weekly*. Our success is driven by our main goal, which is to publish high quality books that will entertain readers as well as make a positive difference in their lives.

Our readers are our most important resource; we value your input, suggestions, and ideas. We'd love to hear from you—after all, we are publishing books for you!

Please stay in touch with us and follow us at:

Facebook: Mango Publishing

Twitter: @MangoPublishing

Instagram: @MangoPublishing

LinkedIn: Mango Publishing

Pinterest: Mango Publishing

Sign up for our newsletter at www.mango.bz and receive a free book!

Join us on Mango's journey to reinvent publishing, one book at a time.

CPSIA information can be obtained
at www.ICGtesting.com
Printed in the USA
JSHW032240270720
6905JS00005B/13

9 781642 502138